25 WALKS

In and Around
GLASGOW

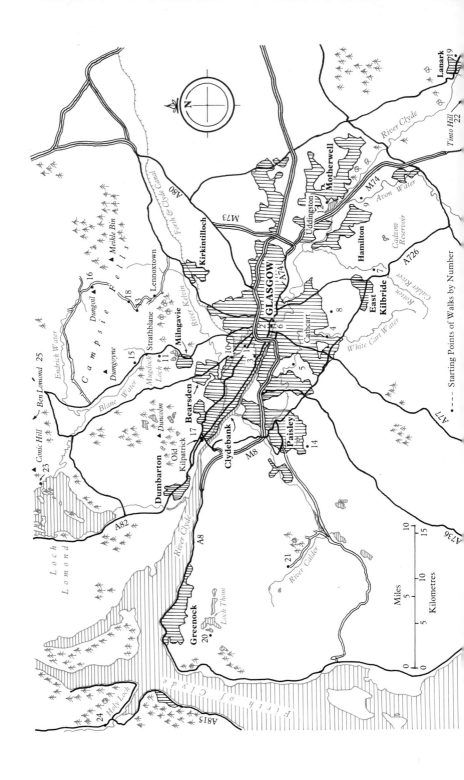

25 WALKS

In and Around
GLASGOW

Alan Forbes

Series Editor: Roger Smith

Strathclyde
Greening
the Conurbation

EDINBURGH:HMSO

First published 1995

Applications for reproduction should be made to HMSO

Acknowledgements

I wish to thank Strathclyde Regional Council and its Planning Committee for agreeing to provide financial support for this book.
Thanks are also due to the Department of Physical Planning for providing valuable information for the text as well as transparencies. I am also grateful to numerous countryside rangers (some of whom I have named) who also supplied important information.
Finally, I would like to thank Roger Smith for inviting me to write this book, and my wife, children and parents for tolerating my repeated absences.

Alan Forbes.

British Library Cataloguing in Publication Data

A catalogue record for this book is available from the British Library

ISBN 0 11 495222 1

CONTENTS

USEFUL INFORMATION

The length of each walk is given in kilometres and miles, but within the text measurements are metric for simplicity. The walks are described in detail and are supported by accompanying maps (study them before you start the walk), so there is little likelihood of getting lost, but if you want a back-up you will find the 1:25 000 Pathfinder Ordnance Survey maps on sale locally.

Every care has been taken to make the descriptions and maps as accurate as possible, but the author and publishers can accept no responsibility for errors, however caused. The countryside is always changing and there will inevitably be alterations to some aspects of these walks as time goes by. The publishers and author would be happy to receive comments and suggested alterations for future editions of the book.

METRIC MEASUREMENTS

At the beginning of each walk, the distance is given in miles and kilometres. Within the text, all measurements are metric for simplicity (and indeed our Ordnance Survey maps are now all metric). However, it was felt that a conversion table might be useful to those readers who, like the author, still tend to think in Imperial terms.

The basic statistic to remember is that one kilometre is five-eighths of a mile. Half a mile is equivalent to 800 metres and a quarter-mile is 400 metres. Below that distance, yards and metres are little different in practical terms.

km	miles
I	0.625
1.6	I
2	1.25
3	1.875
3.2	2
4	2.5
4.8	3
5	3.125
6	3.75
6.4	4
7	4.375
8	5
9	5.625
10	6.25
16	10

INTRODUCTION

Glasgow walks have their share of major historical figures including Mary, Queen of Scots, William Wallace and James Watt, but they also reveal the role played by less celebrated people such as prehistoric fort dwellers, mill workers and miners in shaping the landscape.

The farthest flung walk is Puck's Glen in Argyll. Its inclusion may seem cheeky, but it is a delightful romp, particularly for children, and it is also close to Dunoon, a town traditionally annexed by Glaswegians in summer.

All the walks are intended to be feasible for people new to country walking, and all but the youngest children can tackle many of them. Most of the walks do not need boots, and stout shoes or walking trainers will do. Several of these walks cross country where dogs are not allowed; in other walks dogs must be kept under control.

Glasgow has long been known as a city which has quick access to some of Scotland's most beautiful areas – Loch Lomond, the Trossachs and Glen Coe to name but three.

What is less well known, however, is the amount of lovely scenery right on the city's doorstep. Everyday thousands of people travel to and from the city past the Kilpatrick Hills, the Campsie Fells and along the shores of the Clyde, and possibly do not wonder what they might be like to explore.

This book looks at the countryside around Glasgow and offers suggestions about enjoyable and rewarding days out. It also looks at secluded or surprising corners of the city, often a short distance from well known, bustling streets and shopping centres.

This book also shows that walkers may stand a much greater chance of finding solitude in the hills if they head for somewhere like Meikle Bin or Dungoil in the Campsies than they would on, say, Loch Lomondside where laybys are crowded with hillwalkers' cars.

It is impossible, however, to resist including Ben Lomond in these 25 walks. After all it is Glasgow's own mountain, and a landmark to boast about if seen from the tenement window.

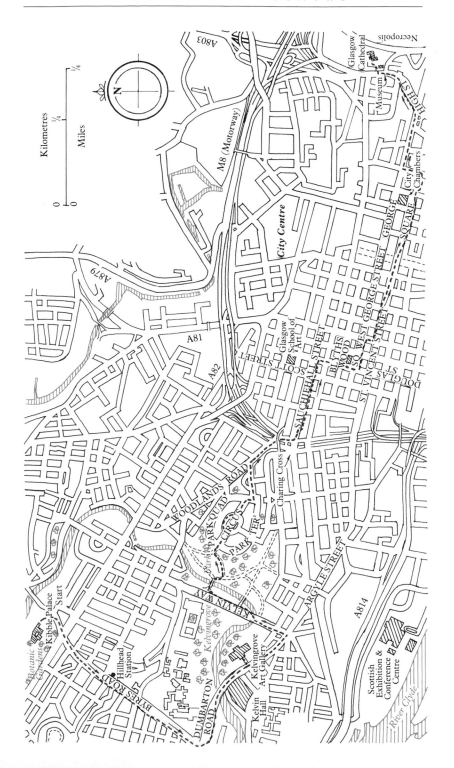

GLASGOW CITY CENTRE

This walk goes against the flow of Glasgow's history. It begins in the West End, where the comfortable Victorian middle classes set up house, and ends at the Cathedral, religious heart of Glasgow from ancient times.

Let's start with a flamboyant send-off from the Kibble Palace in the Botanic Gardens. This crystal flying saucer belonged to a rich Victorian, John Kibble, at Coulport, but was taken to the gardens where it became a focus of gatherings and revelry – which had to be stopped after some of the plants became damaged. More seemly behaviour was exhibited there by William Ewart Gladstone and Benjamin Disraeli when they gave their addresses as rectors of Glasgow University.

From the gardens, head south down Byres Road which is thronged by students, latter-day hippies and other bohemian types. If you still miss that Country Joe and the Fish LP your best friend forgot to return, there's

INFORMATION

Distance: 5 km (3.125 miles)

Start: Botanic Gardens.

Finish: Glasgow Cathedral.

Terrain: City streets and paths. No special footwear needed.

Public transport: Buses or underground from city centre to Kelvingrove.

Refreshments: Wide selection of cafes, pubs, restaurants along route.

Victorian statue in Kibble Palace.

Kelvingrove Art Gallery and Museum.

bound to be a copy in some shop along Byres Road. And if you are looking for a literary lunch, there is Curlers' beside Hillhead Underground station. The bar features a mural of famous customers including the poet Hugh MacDiarmid. Byres Road ends at Partick, one of many Glasgow communities that still retain almost a village intimacy in the face of rushing change and uniformity.

A left turn up Dumbarton Road takes you past two of the city's most famous buildings: the Kelvingrove Art Gallery and Museum to your left and the Kelvin Hall across the road. The Kelvin Hall lost its role as an exhibition centre to the Scottish Exhibition and Conference Centre down by the Clyde, and now houses sports facilities, including a running track, and the city's popular Transport Museum.

There is a story that the architect who designed the art gallery and museum committed suicide when he found the building was the wrong way round. The story is not true, and the exuberance of the building only confirms that. Further on is proof that good architecture, of which Glasgow has plenty, is still being produced. At the important gushet (junction) of Argyle and Sauchiehall Streets stand the Galleries, a modern tenement block that asserts itself strongly.

The route now turns left along Kelvin Way and then right into Kelvingrove Park. Head uphill to Park Terrace and Park Quadrant, the curve of town houses which dominate a wide stretch of Glasgow's west end like a sedate cliff-face.

The Park area, designed in the middle of the last century by Glasgow architect Charles Wilson, is accepted as being the city's most outstanding piece of town design. Poised in front of the terrace, and staring out across Kelvingrove Park, is the equestrian statue of Lord Roberts, Hero of the Empire, who relieved Kandahar and fought the Boers. He would have had a bigger job finding a parking place in what is now a prime business area.

The route continues past the more secluded crescents of Park Circus and down to busy Woodlands Road. This is a major link between the West End and the city centre as well as a focal point, with its local shops, for one of the city's largest Asian communities.

Woodlands Road flies over the M8 motorway to land at Charing Cross and the start of Sauchiehall Street. Around two decades ago, old tenements were demolished to make way for the M8; many Glaswegians regard the motorway as essential for the city's prosperity, but others see it as a brutal slash through the city that encourages traffic congestion and pollution.

Years ago, Sauchiehall Street would have been a first choice for the next stage of the route, all the way down to George Square. A string of chain store and shop frontages on either side have reduced the individuality, though not the popularity, of Glasgow's most famous thoroughfare.

Nevertheless, a 400 m walk along Sauchiehall Street and then a brief turn up to the left at Scott Street takes you to one of the city's architectural gems: Charles Rennie Mackintosh's Glasgow School of Art. Perched on the steep slope of Garnethill, the building has echoes of Scottish tower houses blended into its 'modern' style.

Return to Sauchiehall Street, cross over then head south along Douglas Street to Blythswood Square. Established by the 1830s, this Georgian square was the scene, at number 7, of possibly Glasgow's most famous murder, that of Pierre Emile L'Angelier by his lover, Madeleine Smith, in 1858.

St George's Tron Church in West George Street.

Madeleine succeeded in having the charge of murder by putting arsenic in a cup of cocoa found 'not proven'. She went on to become a successful society hostess in London, and died in her nineties in New York. The descent towards George Square can be made by West George Street, which offers a swooping view down towards St George's Tron Church. A better impression of the city's vibrant commercial life can be had from St Vincent Street. High-rise office blocks, the earliest influenced by New York and Chicago, and the street grid, create a transatlantic atmosphere.

George Square, dominated by the 1880s City Chambers with its Italian marble interior, has long been a rallying point for political protests and demonstrations. In 1993 it was the scene of a joyful gathering when thousands greeted the South African president Nelson Mandela, who had finally arrived in the city to receive the Freedom of Glasgow.

From George Square, the route leads east through the Merchant City, named after the tobacco lords and cotton magnates whose warehouses have been converted into flats. The Merchant City's revival reflects a general growing awareness of Glasgow's rich architectural heritage. The city council has promoted a scheme to floodlight outstanding buildings.

Near the edge of the Merchant City, at the top of the High Street, is Glasgow Cathedral. Built between the 12th and 15th centuries, the cathedral is dedicated to the city's patron saint, Mungo or Kentigern. A new neighbour to the cathedral is the St Mungo Museum of Religious Life.

On a hill behind the Cathedral is the Necropolis, the Victorian burial ground which was modelled on the Père Lachaise in Paris. So near to the city centre, the Necropolis, with its maze of footpaths, offers both a panoramic view of Glasgow and a secluded world of lavish monuments and simple gravestones standing side by side.

George Square.

The Necropolis is the last resting place of many who made their mark, from the Tennent family of brewing fame to William Miller, who penned the popular children's song Wee Willie Winkie. One of the people interred securely at the Necropolis was no respector of graves. Granville Sharp Pattison was a medical teacher who relied on 'sack 'em up boys' to provide him with bodies for dissection. When the teeth of a newly-dead woman were found in his rooms he was put on trial, but he wriggled free with a 'not proven' verdict and went on to a successful career in New York.

The Necropolis has always been a popular place for a quiet walk. It has been closed for repairs to dangerous tombs although at the time of writing, arrangements were being made to provide limited access to parts of the Necropolis. Enquiries about access should be made to Glasgow District's parks department.

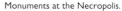

Monuments at the Necropolis.

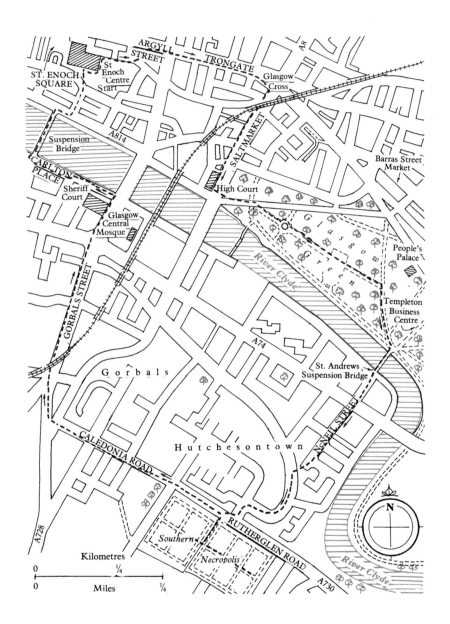

CROSSRIVER WALK

The emphasis of this walk is on a changing Glasgow, communities which have been radically transformed several times over and are now coming back for a new lease of life.

The walk begins in St Enoch Square, beside Argyle Street. St Enoch was actually a woman, St Thenew, who gave birth to St Mungo or St Kentigern, future patron saint of Glasgow. The square formed the site of railway station and hotel.

These were demolished, causing ill-feeling among many citizens, and the large site was left unused. Eventually, plans were approved for Glasgow's first modern indoor shopping mall. The new St Enoch Centre was claimed to be Europe's largest glass-covered shopping centre. Looking like a crystal Toblerone bar, the mall dominates the north bank of the Clyde.

Walk east along Argyle Street and the Trongate to Glasgow Cross, gathering place of Hogmanay revellers and the hub of the old city where witches were burned, stagecoaches exchanged passengers and wealthy merchants enjoyed a promenade. Turn right and walk down Saltmarket for about 250 m to the High Court, where countless murderers and other malefactors have come to judgement. Behind the

INFORMATION

Distance: 3.5 km (2 miles).

Start and finish: St Enoch Square.

Terrain: City streets and paths. No special footwear needed.

Refreshments: Shops and cafes on route.

Further reading: Two reasonably priced books provide excellent information on the city walks: Central Glasgow, an Illustrated Architectural Guide, by Charles McKean and David and Frank Walker (Mainstream), and The Glasgow Graveyard Guide by Jimmy Black (Saint Andrew Press).

Winter Gardens at rear of People's Palace in Glasgow Green.

court is Paddy's Market. It has long been rumoured that the city's 'modernisers' would like to see the back of this rather unprepossessing flea market. Nevertheless, the traders have been able to show the likes of the now defunct Briggait market nearby how to run a business.

Cross over Saltmarket and enter the city's most hallowed open space, Glasgow Green. This is the place where the Glasgow Fair was traditionally held, as well as political rallies by Red Clydesiders. This is also where James Watt went for a stroll and hit on an idea which achieved a breakthrough in developing the steam engine. The green has traditionally been a place of recreation for ordinary Glaswegians. Continuing loyalty to the area among citizens was shown recently when a plan to build a road tunnel under the green was withdrawn after loud protest.

Glasgow's strong tradition of working-class activism is reflected at the green in the People's Palace, a museum which concentrates on the life of ordinary citizens. Life changes – just consider the old Templeton carpet factory near the People's Palace. This was the biggest carpet factory in Britain, supplying luxury liners such as the Queen Mary as well as princes and maharajas.

The Barras street market.

Previous designs for the building were rejected by the corporation. But when an exotic design decorated with brick and tile to resemble the Doge's Palace in Venice was submitted, the city fathers approved. There was a disaster in 1889 when the elaborate wall collapsed, killing 29 women workers. The builder was blamed for failing to tie the wall to the building properly. The factory nevertheless went from strength to strength until 1968, when falling orders forced closure. The factory is now the Templeton Business Centre, providing fertile ground for new, small enterprises.

A short distance north of the business centre is the legendary Barras street market. There may not be many pins or anchors these days but there is still a wide variety of items for sale. If you want to buy china, clothes, furnishings or fittings at knock-down prices, this is where to come.

Return to Glasgow Green and then cross to the south side of the Clyde by the St Andrews suspension bridge. You are now in Hutchesontown. This area, like neighbouring Gorbals, exchanged overcrowded slums for windy, inhospitable high flats. Most of these blocks have been demolished to make way for more traditional low-rise houses with gardens.

The route follows McNeil Street, past new housing and refurbished flats on one side and Allied Distillers' Strathclyde Distillery on the other. Cross Rutherglen Road where it joins Caledonia Road and enter the castle-like portal of the Southern Necropolis. Established from the 1840s, this cemetery was laid out in three large sections to serve a burgeoning population without posing a public health risk, unlike previous, overcrowded graveyards. Gravestones and monuments provide a fascinating insight into a community which was absorbing many of Glasgow's immigrants. The most famous person buried here was probably Sir Thomas Lipton, the millionaire grocer. The memorial to the famous Glasgow architect, Alexander 'Greek' Thomson, is also here.

Rowing on the Clyde seen from the St Andrew's suspension bridge.

The route heads west along Caledonia Road to the 'Greek' Thomson church at the junction with Gorbals Street. Gutted by fire in 1965 this church is a forlorn shell that still evokes admiration. Schemes to restore it have come to nothing.

Heading back to the city, the route passes another religious landmark, the Glasgow Central Mosque. The golden, onion-shaped dome brings welcome colour to a stretch of riverfront that has only recently begun to be appreciated again for its architectural possibilities. From the mosque, cross Gorbals Street to the new Sheriff Court and follow the riverside past the 19th century terrace at Carlton Place to the pretty suspension bridge. The bridge will take you back across the Clyde to St Enoch Square.

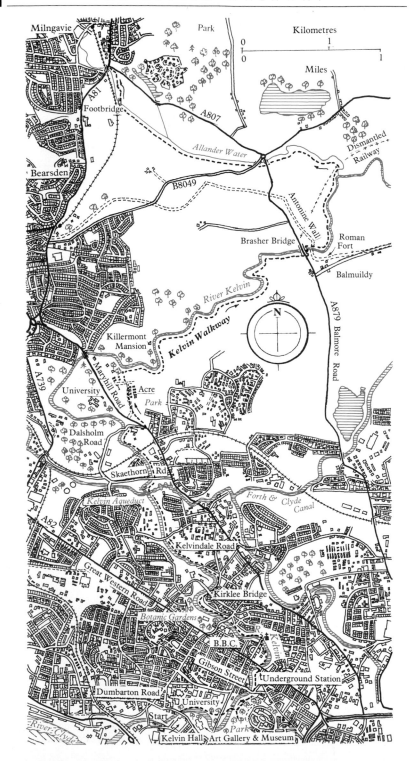

THE KELVIN WALKWAY

L et us haste to Kelvin Grove, Bonnie Lassie O,
Through its mazes let us rove, Bonnie Lassie O.

The composer, Dr Thomas Lyle, an obscure Paisley-born surgeon who died in 1858, may be long forgotten but the song is not. This sentimental evocation of supposedly more sedate times paints a surprisingly accurate picture of the 'hollow dingle (deep dell) side' still to be found on the Kelvin's banks within the Glasgow boundary.

Aside from the justly famous Kelvingrove Park itself, long stretches of beautiful, wooded riverside nestle below the tall Victorian bridges that carry traffic through the city's West End. The Kelvin flows for 21 miles from the Kilsyth Hills to Partick, where it joins the Clyde.

INFORMATION

Distance: 13 km (8 miles).

Start: Kelvin Hall.

Finish: Milngavie railway station.

Terrain: Roads and tracks. Flat, easy going but overgrown and possibly muddy in places. Strong footwear recommended.

Public transport: Frequent buses from city centre to Kelvin Hall. Regular trains from Milngavie to Glasgow Queen Street.

Refreshments: Selection of pubs and cafes in Milngavie.

Where walkway passes under Belmont Street bridge, in Glasgow's Kelvinside.

This junction is where the Glasgow bakers were granted permission by the Regent Moray in 1568 to take over the running of the city's flourmills from the Crown. This may seem scant recognition for the citizens' part in routing the troops of Mary, Queen of Scots at Langside, but the city was well pleased to be rid of the exorbitant tax levied by the crown.

The walk starts on Dumbarton Road, opposite the Kelvin Hall, and initially follows the right bank of the Kelvin, passing the Kelvingrove Art Gallery and Museum on the opposite bank, with Glasgow University and its soaring tower dominating Gilmorehill high on the left. In spate, the River Kelvin at this point loses its douce charm and can be very challenging for canoeists. Cross the treelined Kelvin Way, which carries traffic through Kelvingrove, then enter Kelvingrove Park by crossing a footbridge over the river. Inside the park, head uphill a short distance to inspect the Stewart Fountain. This commemorates Lord Provost Robert Stewart, who met the burgeoning city's greatest need by initiating the clean water supply from Loch Katrine.

Turn left, walk under the bridge which leads to Gibson Street, and enter a grassy area leading to Kelvinbridge Underground Station. Before the station, cross a footbridge to the left bank and walk under Great Western Road and Belmont Street bridges, the latter dominated by the Stevenson Memorial Church, where the Boys Brigade held its first meeting over 100 years ago.

The path recrosses the Kelvin yet again and passes the remains of an old mill, with the BBC's Queen Margaret Drive studios on the opposite bank. Along here, it is easy to appreciate how much the Victorians valued open space in their cities. Not only is this stretch rich in trees and grassy verges, it also has direct access, via a footbridge, to the tropical plants in the nearby Kibble Palace at the Botanic Gardens.

A short distance farther on, at the towering Kirklee Bridge, is another example of Victorian luxury. The bridge is almost entirely of red sandstone but four pillars on either side of the river are of polished red granite, like

a lavish flourish of the builder's signature. Farther on, the
path rises above the river and goes past three tower
blocks of flats on the right. After the last block, cut down
to Kelvindale Road and cross over to the continuation of
Kelvin Walkway (indicated by the walkway's sign, a
green duck on a yellow disc).

Take the path that leads left, back towards the Kelvin,
and then follow the river along the path that is bounded
on the right by a low wall. Through the trees the bulk of
the Kelvin Aqueduct can be seen. Before it, however, are
the uprights of a dismantled railway bridge. Look
carefully and you may spot a cormorant preening itself on
an upright of the bridge.

Following Allander Water
to Milgavnie.

Walk through the arch below the aqueduct, which
carries the Forth and Clyde Canal, and then under a
small bridge, ignoring a narrow track that leads left
towards the river. Go past a landscaped area, under
another large bridge at Skaethorn Road, then follow the
right-hand curve of the river past another landscaped
area. Ahead, on the opposite bank, is a low cliff. Soon,
when you enter a small wood, another outcrop rises on
your right.

The route abandons the Kelvin at Dalsholm Road, because no access is permitted through the Garscube Estate, now owned by Glasgow University. Walk up Dalsholm Road, cross Maryhill Road and enter Maryhill Park. The view from the top of the park stretches from the Campsies in the east round to the Kilpatrick Hills and much of the city while, overhead, airliners wait their turn to land at Glasgow Airport.

Head downhill, through the Acre housing scheme or farther east, to return to the Kelvin. The riverbank is behind a line of trees beyond a field. The easiest way is to head towards Killermont mansion, the clubhouse of Glasgow Golf Club on the opposite bank.

Just outside Glasgow, now in open country.

Rejoin the route and cross a stile into woodland. Here, much work has been done to upgrade the path and prevent erosion. Out of the wood, head over to the embankment holding back the river. The track continues for about 1.5 km across open country, with a view of the Campsies, particularly the rhino horn of Dumgoyne, emerging to the north.

To the right, seagulls betray the fact that the landscaped slope overlooking the path is the edge of a landfill dump. Up ahead, traffic can be seen on Balmore Road, crossing the Kelvin. There is no need to join the vehicles to cross the river. Instead, when you get to the bridge, cross over and use the footbridge, built in 1993.

This welcome addition to the Kelvin Walkway is called the Brasher Bridge because it was funded partly by the Christopher

Brasher Trust as well as Strathclyde Regional Council and Glasgow District Council. Descend a wooden staircase and go through a stile. Within a few yards the line of the Antonine Wall is reached (just south of the river is the site of the large Roman fort at Balmuildy).

The going is now rather rough. Keep to the embankment, and as you swing round a left-hand bend in the river you come upon a pair of clever 'alternative' stiles, employed to protect a route that cattle use to get to the water. These protected openings have two hinged, upright bars, connected to posts by chains. The bars swing apart to let walkers through, then automatically swing shut.

Continuing along the embankment, the route joins the right bank of the Allander Water where it flows into the Kelvin. Stay on the embankment and approach the line of a dismantled railway. During 1994, new sewers were being installed at this section of the route, but care was taken to preserve access for walkers. Steps were provided over a fence and the route was directed through a safe part of the works site bounded by high fencing.

Farther along the embankment, which takes you back towards Balmore Road, another potential hindrance for walkers was dealt with in admirable fashion by the farmer. The record rainfall of March 1994 had gouged a deep, muddy channel from a field into the river. Conditions improved considerably, however, when a ramp was provided for the farmer's cattle – and walkers.

The route crosses Balmore Road, just outside the Glasgow boundary, and the B8049 into Bearsden. Rejoin the Allander Water, noting two walkway signs. One warns against bringing dogs, because of grazing animals. The other shows that the duck has been transmogrified into a heron (a wee touch of satire, maybe, from good Bearsden and Milngavie folk who refuse to be called Glaswegians).

You are now on the home stretch: the route follows an attractive line for about a mile along the right bank with fields sloping down from Crow Hill. Close to Milngavie, cross the Allander Water by a footbridge erected in 1990 by visiting Royal Engineers in memory of Staff Sergeant Jim Prescott, who died in the Falklands Campaign.

The route joins Glasgow Road in the town. Head uphill, turn left into Station Road and arrive at the pretty Victorian station, which has frequent services back to Glasgow.

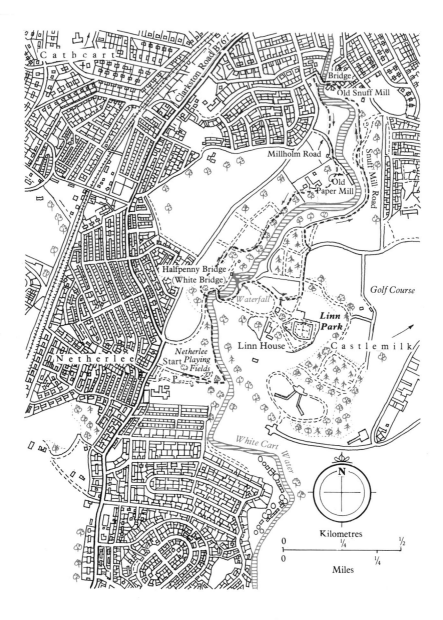

LINN PARK

Fancy a pinch of snuff? Well, you're too late, as this walk will reveal.

Linn Park, like its neighbours, Pollok and Rouken Glen parks, demonstrates how well off the south side of Glasgow is for open spaces rich in wildlife. The three parks have joined in the Carts River Valleys project. This project is a recent development in Strathclyde Regional Council's Greening the Conurbation strategy which seeks to improve the environment of the Clyde valley.

The Carts River Valleys project involves Strathclyde along with Glasgow, Eastwood and Renfrew district councils, and Scottish Natural Heritage in a programme of path upgrading, landscaping and woodland conservation. The project is targeted on areas surrounding the White Cart Water, Black Cart Water, River Gryffe and some of their tributaries.

In the case of Linn Park, the river is the White Cart. This flows through the middle of the park's 212 acres of mixed woodland and parkland. The White Cart was in fact the cause of Linn Park getting its name. A Victorian owner called the park after the waterfall or linn that is a dramatic feature when the river is in spate.

INFORMATION

Distance: 3.2 km (2 miles).

Start and finish: Netherlee playing fields car park, Linnpark Avenue, off Clarkston Road.

Terrain: All on good roads or paths. No special footwear needed.

Public transport: The Snuff Mill Road entrance is only 250m from Cathcart Station (frequent trains from Glasgow Central). From the station walk south along Castle Road to Snuff Mill Road.

Linn at Linn Park.

Linn Park lies only five miles from Glasgow city centre. It is surrounded by three communities, Netherlee, Cathcart and Castlemilk, yet it remains a sanctuary not only for wildlife but urban dwellers of the human variety who crave beautiful scenery and peace and quiet.

The park's main gate is on Clarkston Road. There are no parking facilities in Linn Park but motorists can take the first left after the main gates into Linnpark Avenue and leave their cars in the Netherlee playing fields car park.

Follow a track that borders the playing fields and runs down to the trees and bushes on the left bank of the White Cart. Turn left along the riverside path that soon leads into Linn Park. Ahead you will soon make out the pretty, white Halfpenny Bridge which crosses the river. Also known as the White Bridge it was built in 1835, making it the oldest cast iron bridge in Glasgow. It is thought it got its Halfpenny title from the round holes in each span.

Halfpenny Bridge.

Cross the bridge and walk along an attractive avenue of lime trees to Linn House, the mansion that was built as a summer home for the wealthy Campbell family who bought the estate and gave it its name.

The park's countryside rangers are based in the mansion. The staff are part of Glasgow District Council's team of five full-time and three seasonal rangers also responsible for Pollok Park, Cathkin Braes and Netherton Braes.

The route heads north from the mansion along a tarmac road that skirts the trees overlooking the river on the left, and Linn Park golf course high on the right. About 300 m from the mansion, the road swings to the right. At this point, follow a tarmac path that leads towards the river.

The path at first goes downhill by beech trees, then switches to a gravel surface past an open grassy area. Back into the woods, the path runs underneath a canopy of mainly oak trees and rhododendron, then you encounter an overhanging rock wall to your right, and a sign warning of possible loose rocks. At this point walkers can make out the buildings that mark the end of the route and also explain the reference to snuff. The path emerges onto the attractive and secluded Snuff Mill Road.

The buildings on the right bank of the White Cart were originally the old Cathcart meal mill and the mill cottage. The mill switched to cardboard production in the early 1800s, and snuff milling shortly after. As you cross the picturesque little bridge to the left bank of the river, you may notice that much work has been done to convert the mill buildings into houses. Concrete shuttering has also been erected to protect the property from flooding.

Looking down White Cart from bridge beside old Snuff Mill.

Re-enter the park by a flight of steps and follow the left bank upriver, crossing Millholm Road. The path gradually drops closer to the riverbank. Kingfishers may be spotted flitting through the mainly deciduous trees, including oak, ash, elm and beech. More likely you will see a 'tree rat' – a grey squirrel – scampering from branch to branch.

As the path approaches the Halfpenny Bridge, there is still one treat to enjoy. The linn announces itself audibly well before it can be seen, but after heavy rainfall, its roar can fill the river valley for some distance.

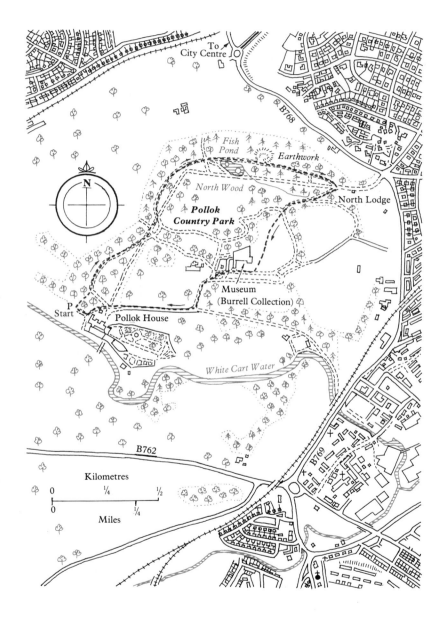

To
City Centre

B708

Fish
Pond

Earthwork

North Wood

*Pollok
Country Park*

North Lodge

N

Museum
(Burrell Collection)

P
Start

Pollok House

White Cart Water

B762

B769

Kilometres

0   ¼   ½

0   ¼

Miles

POLLOK COUNTRY PARK

Many people pay thousands of pounds to move out of the city for a home in the countryside. Some discover their rural idyll, but others may find their desire for wide open spaces constrained by hostile 'no trespass' signs and rolling acres given over to monoculture forests and agribusiness.

Pollok Park, however, is a bit like Mother Nature's version of Glasgow's Barras market. You want it? You got it! You want foxes, you get foxes, and not the timid, country type either. If you live around Pollok Park, expect a gallus Glasgow fox to be around your door some morning to inspect the wheely bin. And don't forget to keep the cat in.

Pollok must be the only country park that features two art collections (Pollok House and the Burrell Collection) on its list of attractions as well as acres of woodland and parkland. Most walkers start from Pollok House. Unlike the Burrell's, the car park at Pollok House is free and less busy. More importantly, Pollok House feels more on the woodland doorstep than the Burrell, and the countryside rangers' centre (where guided walks can be arranged) and demonstration gardens are in its grounds.

This walk is only one of an almost infinite variety of routes that can be selected in the park. Leave Pollok

INFORMATION

Distance: 3.2 km (2 miles).

Start and finish: Car park at Pollok House.

Terrain: Good paths, although wood exploring can be a muddy exercise.

Public transport: Pollokshaws West station is 200 m from the main entrance to the park. Regular bus services also to and from the city centre.

Refreshments: Cafes in Pollok House and Burrell Collection (which also serves full meals and alcohol).

Pollok House.

Carvings at Pollok House.

House car park, turn left along the tarmac road and then almost immediately swing right up a path going across rough grassland by silver birch trees.

The grassland here is a beautiful flower meadow in early summer, and it leads on to another tarmac road which provides flat, comfortable going for wheelchair visitors. Turn left along this road, and go past a broad grassy avenue (The Glade) running up to the right towards the Burrell Collection.

The road may be fringed by rhododendron blossom among old oaks, and you will soon come to the fish pond on the right. This has been cleaned out, and mallards and moorhens raise their broods on the small islands. A new path and picnic area have also made the pond area more amenable to visitors.

A short distance along the road, hidden behind the trees on the left, is a probable medieval defensive ringwork surrounded by a deep, now leaf-filled, ditch or moat. There are traces of inner and outer banks formed by earth and other material from the ditch.

For its full length the road skirts the North Wood. This must have been a paradise for generations of children who were able to explore, unhindered by adults. Little wonder neighbouring communities such as Corkerhill have protested against plans to extend the M77 motorway between them and Pollok Country Park, leaving restricted access.

The road reaches the North Lodge, at the north-eastern edge of the park. The lodge was built for the Maxwells, to whom Pollok belonged for 700 years from the 13th Century. You are now presented with three paths to follow. Take the middle one which soon crosses a bridge and then leads to a crossroads. Go straight over, make your way through the horse chestnut trees to the edge of the wood, and prepare yourself for the view. A broad stretch of parkland rolls downhill to a line of trees and then blocks of high flats on the skyline. Over to the right, with a glass curtain wall mirroring trees, stands the Burrell Collection. A gazebo built at the top of the hill in the summer of 1994 is a good viewpoint for the Burrell.

Opened in 1983, the gallery quickly became one of Scotland's most popular tourist attractions (some years the most popular). The striking design of the building, its setting against the woodland and the collection of art and historical objects come together in an irresistible combination. The collection was gifted to Glasgow by Sir William Burrell, a wealthy shipowner.

Sir William's insistence that his precious and delicate collection should be housed in a country setting well away from the smoke of industrial Glasgow posed a difficult problem for Glasgow Corporation. The problem was not to be solved until the Clean Air Act was passed and a member of the Maxwell family gifted Pollok House and estate to the city.

Yet again there is a choice of route for the next, and final, leg of the walk. A longer way takes you along the right bank of the White Cart Water. Here you may glimpse a kingfisher flitting past the willow trees. The kingfisher is the symbol of the Carts River Valleys Project, started by Strathclyde Regional Council to protect and extend wildlife habitats in the south side of Glasgow and Renfrewshire.

Your route, however, follows the main avenue which runs between fields occupied by some of the City of Glasgow's 70 Highland cattle, always popular with children. Other well-loved large animals, two heavy horses, may be found in the stables of Pollok House which is at the end of the avenue. The horses carry visitors around the park on a wagon.

Pollok House.

The walk ends in the grounds of Pollok House, which overlooks the White Cart. The house was originally built in the 1750s but later extended. The homes of estate workers were demolished because they spoiled the view from Pollok House, and the families were rehoused in nearby Shawlands. Such was the price of elegant living.

If your feet are not too muddy, you can enter the house and view the painting collection which specialises in the works of Spanish artists including Goya.

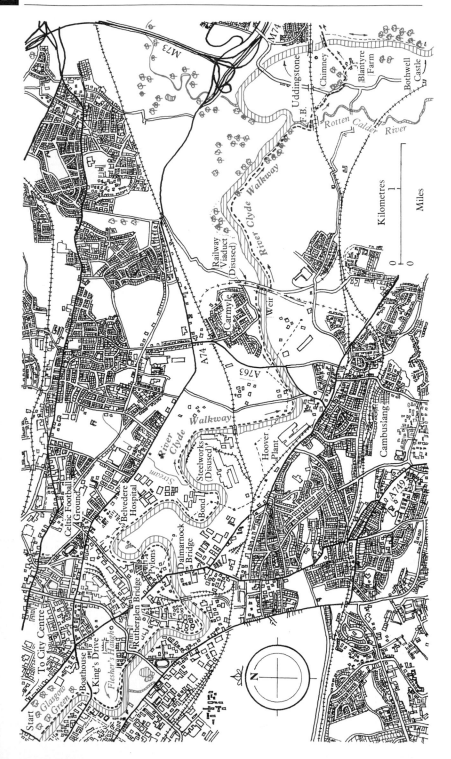

THE CLYDE WALKWAY

I f rivers were judged purely on vital statistics, then the Clyde wouldn't rate a second look. At 105 miles, it is half as long as the Thames, and where it runs through Glasgow it is possible to 'chuck' a stone from one bank to the other.

Yet the Clyde has always been an important river in Scottish terms, and for a long time was a great river in world terms. The glory days of shipbuilding may be gone but, depending upon what stretch you are on, the Clyde can be ugly, beautiful, boisterous or peaceful.

The route described here is the longest in this book, but is one of the simplest to follow. The walk can also be done in bite-sized chunks as, for much of the way, obvious exits to bus routes back to the city centre can be found. Children who are used to a day's hillwalking should be able to tackle the full route, which involves level going apart from an easy scramble up to a disused railway viaduct.

INFORMATION

Distance: 14 km (8.75 miles).

Start: Glasgow Green.

Finish: Bothwell Castle.

Terrain: Pavement then tracks, with brief scrambles on to and down from disused railway viaduct at Carmyle.

Public transport: Regular trains from Uddingston station to Glasgow Central.

Right bank of Clyde near Bothwell Castle.

For the purpose of extending this walk out from the city without including too much of the city itself, a fitting start may be made at Glasgow Green, once the place for a promenade or open air meeting. Walk through the Green, and pass the Glasgow Humane Society's boathouse. On the opposite side of the path is the society's house, which is home to George and Ann Parsonage. Their father, Ben, rescued over 1,000 people from the river, and recovered a similar number of bodies. George has carried on his father's work, often in extremely hazardous conditions.

Cross King's Drive and enter Fleshers' Haugh, the area where livestock was grazed before being slaughtered for local consumption. It was here that Bonnie Prince Charlie reviewed his army of Highlanders less than four months before their defeat at Culloden in 1746.

Take the broad path that follows the curve of the right bank and then goes under Rutherglen Bridge. The path is now quite narrow, posing a peculiar problem if the walk is done on holidays or weekends. This stretch of the river is popular for rowing practice, and for every

boat that skims along the river there is a coach cycling in pursuit. Some coaches do not seem to bother much about avoiding anyone who shares the path with them. They simply speed past, their eyes on the water, bellowing technical phrases such as: 'I want to see a big puddle coming off that blade.'

Disused Carmyle railway viaduct.

Waterfowl are plentiful on the river long before the attractive, painted iron railway and road bridges at Dalmarnock are reached. After the road bridge the path goes under electricity pylons. Do not follow the track down to the riverbank because planks on a platform over the river have been removed and there are holes in the ground. The path meanders on, passing high flats, and the floodlights of Celtic Park appear on the skyline ahead.

The river does a U-turn and for about 300 m the route is marred by an ugly, brown corrugated iron fence, intended to keep intruders out of the grounds of Belvidere Hospital. Someone, however, has managed to pull back a corner of the fence, so a wire security fence would be more effective and discreet. After this eyesore, however, the path gets into attractive, open countryside, and goes along the top of a wooded embankment which curves with the river. You soon approach a large Allied Distillers whisky bond.

While crossing underneath pylons, ignore a path that leads to the right; instead, stick to the path as it briefly veers away from the river. The path returns to the riverbank and goes by the bond. At the corner of the security fencing, go down off the embankment and cross a stream. Follow a sharp bend where the river runs fast and where a disused steelworks sits on the opposite bank.

Go under a stonebuilt railway bridge and a modern road bridge, then go between three yellow posts to continue along the path. Remember there are no free flights in this journey as you pass the Hoover plant at Cambuslang on the opposite bank.

The path goes under two more bridges before arriving at Carmyle. Go past the weir on this particularly attractive part of the river, then clamber up the embankment and onto the disused railway viaduct. Cross the viaduct and then take the obvious track down to the left bank. Now you are in real countryside: as the sound of the weir recedes, the racket from crows and sheep takes over. The route follows an idyllic 2 km across fields, alongside the wooded riverbank, and then you enter a beech wood on a steep slope overlooking the river.

When you arrive at the small Rotten Calder river, don't cross over. Instead cut south away from the Clyde for about 300 m. Keep high above the river and a tangle of thornbushes, follow the track through the field and a fence which takes you to a stile. Trend left downhill until the track becomes more obvious and leads, by stone steps, down to the Rotten Calder (apparently named after its reddish appearance).

Cross the river by a footbridge beside a railway bridge. Cross a stile and turn right onto a farm road which goes under the railway. Follow the rough motor track that swings uphill to the left and joins a tarmac road. In the gloaming the motorway interchanges to the north put on an impressive light display.

Join the Blantyre Farm Road, turn right, walk a few yards (beware of fast traffic on this short stretch) then cross over, go through a kissing gate and follow the obvious path, signed to Blantyre Farm. Go past the farm and follow a track downhill with a tall chimney to your left. Rejoin the Clyde and cross the river by a lime green footbridge. If time is short, you can follow the track for less than 100 m and take a left fork which leads into Uddingston and the railway station nearby. The perfect ending, however, is to continue along the riverside for about 800 m to Bothwell Castle.

Bothwell was one of the great castles of Scotland, fought over by the Scots and English during the Wars of Independence. In 1301, the English besieged the castle with a huge wheeled, wooden tower. Thirty-six years later its owner, Sir Andrew de Moray, demolished the outer half of the great donjon tower to deny the castle to the English. The inner-half of the tower remains as part of the massive red sandstone ramparts which dominate this beautiful, wooded part of the Clyde.

Bothwell Castle on right bank of Clyde.

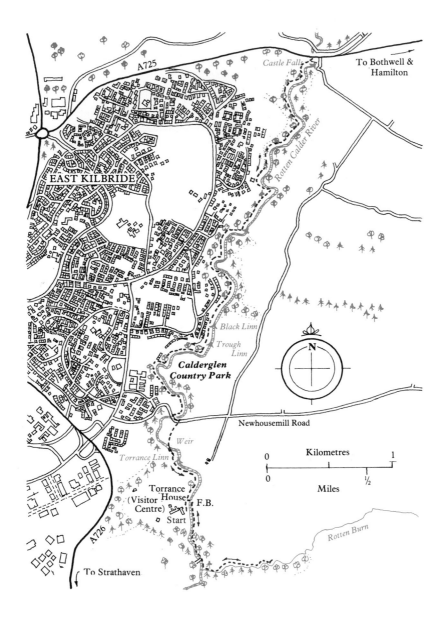

To Bothwell & Hamilton

Castle Falls

A725

Rotten Calder River

EAST KILBRIDE

N

Black Linn

Trough Linn

Calderglen Country Park

Newhousemill Road

Weir

Torrance Linn

Torrance (Visitor House Centre)

F.B.

Start

A726

Rotten Burn

To Strathaven

Kilometres
0 1

0 1/2
Miles

CALDERGLEN COUNTRY PARK

From this distance in time, it is easy to believe that new towns were drawn on blank sheets of paper rather than built on real pieces of land. East Kilbride in Lanarkshire, for instance, was Scotland's first new town, acquiring its population from an overcrowded Glasgow. But the ground on which the newcomers' homes were built had long been part of the fabric of history.

The old parish, one of several Kilbrides in Scotland, was given the prefix East long ago to distinguish it from the more westerly parish of Kilbride in Ayrshire. East Kilbride's neighbouring parish of Torrance, central to this walk, was annexed before the Reformation and legally incorporated with East Kilbride by the presbytery of Glasgow in 1589. Torrance House, the focal point of Calderglen Country Park, stands on the left bank of the Rotten Calder river which forms the

INFORMATION

Distance: 8 km (5 miles).

Start and finish: Car park at Torrance House. From East Kilbride town centre, head east following signs for Strathaven and Calderglen Country Park. Entrance to country park off A726 road to Strathaven.

Terrain: Undulating riverside path. Strong footwear advised, especially in wet conditions.

Public transport: Regular trains from Glasgow Central to East Kilbride, then Strathaven buses passing the park entrance.

Refreshments: Cafe in Torrance House.

Rotten Burn.

eastern boundary of East Kilbride. The central part of the building is the tower house, built in 1605 with wings added over a century and a half later.

The development corporation took over Torrance House in 1947 to plan the new town, but vandalism and neglect almost resulted in the building being demolished. In the late 1970s, however, East Kilbride District Council decided to set up a country park, and part of Torrance House became the visitor centre. The country park is a popular recreation area with a golf course, sports centre and a children's zoo.

The big informal attraction is the lovely riverside, with woodland walks along a 5 km stretch. From the Torrance House visitor centre, follow 'nature trail' signs along a path that skirts round the edge of the large lawn in front of the house.

Where the path splits among the bushes, take the left turn in the direction of the sign for the adventure playground. Go downhill, guarded by safety barriers from the steep slope on the right, until you arrive at the left bank of the Rotten Calder. Now follow the sign indicating 'Torrance Linn 350 metres'.

Rotten Calder river below visitor centre.

The track crosses a field and runs beside ash trees growing by the river. Arrive at Torrance Linn, an attractive weir, and then continue for a short distance to the stepping stones which take you across the river to the wildflower meadow. The stones are easy to cross except in wet weather, when they can be slimy.

Cross the meadow to Newhousemill Road. The bridge here used to be a traffic bottleneck, but piles of sand were dumped on the road in spring 1994 to stop vehicles using the bridge after floodwater had torn masonry out of one of its piers. Cross the bridge and rejoin the path downriver on the left bank. The path skirts round waste ground, swings uphill away from the river and continues through a mature spruce plantation.

Much has been done on pathwork, with earth banks being shored up and the path itself covered in roadmetal for stability and drainage. Being a linear walk, the route can be as long as you wish to make it. The route leads 4 km from Torrance House to where the A725 road crosses over the river on its way to Bothwell and Hamilton. The path takes you through predominantly beech and other deciduous trees, at times sticking close to the bank and at others, sweeping up onto vantage points overlooking the waterfalls of Trough Linn, Black Linn and Castle Falls.

Wildflowers in riverside woods.

The last-named falls are close to the site of Calderwood Castle, a Victorian gothic mansion that was demolished in 1951. The mansion was built on the site of previous castles, said to have belonged first to a Calderwood family and then to a branch of the Maxwell family of Pollok beside Glasgow. In 1904 the Scottish Co-operative Wholesale Society bought the estate and opened the grounds to the public.

At Calderwood Castle there is a small nature trail with planting including a giant sequoia. Returning to Torrance House, ignore the path that led down to the river from the house. Instead cross the footbridge and follow the right bank of the Rotten Calder upstream to its junction with the Rotten Burn. The Burn can then be followed for a short distance through the woods.

Although the path here becomes gradually narrower and more slippy it does take you into a less frequented and particularly attractive corner of the country park.

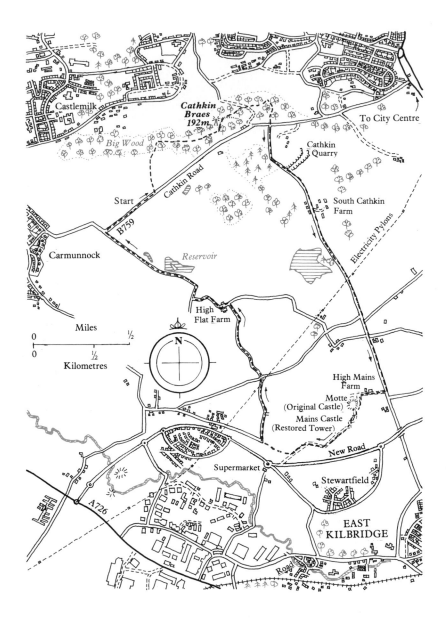

Castlemilk

Cathkin Braes 192m

To City Centre

Cathkin Quarry

Big Wood

Cathkin Road

Start

South Cathkin Farm

B759

Carmunnock

Reservoir

Electricity Pylons

High Flat Farm

Miles

0   ½

0   ½

Kilometres

N

High Mains Farm

Motte (Original Castle)

Mains Castle (Restored Tower)

New Road

Supermarket

Stewartfield

A726

🦌 EAST KILBRIDGE

Road

CATHKIN BRAES

This is not so much a wild walk as a walk on the slightly weird side. It features possibly the best Glasgow panorama, close links with two historical characters who met particularly messy ends . . . and a forced detour past a supermarket.

At one point, the route is less than 8 km from the centre of Glasgow, yet it includes a little-known network of attractive country lanes and tracks. The walk follows a circuit starting from the B759 Cathkin Road just over 1 km north-east of Carmunnock. If you don't have a car, take the bus to the attractive village of Carmunnock, otherwise park your car at one of several laybys on the B759.

INFORMATION

Distance: 8 km (5 miles).

Start and finish: Laybys on B759 north-east of Carmunnock.

Terrain: All on tracks or through fields. Strong footwear advised, and be prepared for some muddy going.

Public transport: Buses from Glasgow city centre to Carmunnock.

Public transport: Strathclyde Buses services from St Enoch Square to East Kilbride stop at Carmunnock.

Refreshments: None en route. Nearest in Carmunnock or East Kilbride.

View over Glasgow from summit of Cathkin Braes. Castlemilk in foreground.

On the north side of the road, cross an expanse of rough grassland to the Big Wood. This consists mainly of mature beech, but also includes oak, larch, Scots pine and sycamore. As you follow the wood northeast, glimpses of high flats in Castlemilk and more distant parts of Glasgow begin to open up, a promise of sights to come.

What impresses about the Big Wood is that it seems to get on with its own life. Grey squirrels flit around the branches, trees die and lean against their neighbours or fall to the ground to rot. Some time before leaving the wood you will see the police radio mast on top of Cathkin Braes. When you arrive at the spot, 192 m above sea level, you may be disappointed by the eyesore caused by the mast and its neighbouring brick building and security fence.

Turn your back on the intrusion and look at Glasgow, spread out below like a relief map. The view has improved recently following major improvements to houses in Castlemilk. Farther out, Glasgow Cathedral can be seen, and then the Campsies and Ben Lomond on the northern skyline. It is easy to see why Glasgow City Council wants to raise £2.2 million to turn the Cathkin Braes area into a country park with a visitor centre.

From the vantage point one of the historical characters, Mary, Queen of Scots, is believed to have observed her forces being defeated at the Battle of Langside. After this she escaped to England, was imprisoned and then beheaded for plotting against Elizabeth I. It has been suggested that Mary viewed the battle from a neighbouring hill, but there was nothing to prevent her moving round on horseback. Only at the very end of her life would she have been in two places at once.

Continue along the grassy plateau to a viewfinder and go down to a lower, grassy area. Follow a row of swings beside the wood. Before the last swing, turn right towards trees bordering the B759. Pass through a gap

in the metal fence, cross the road and walk up the side road marked Works Access. Beyond the entrance to the Cathkin Quarry Coup (dump) your eyes will be drawn to trees on the right rather than to the coup on the left, which is being grass seeded.

Horses in morning mist at South Cathkin Farm.

The route leads to South Cathkin Farm then follows a track towards electricity pylons on the skyline. The low part of this track can be something of an obstacle course with mud in the middle and hawthorn hedges on each side.

Cross a gate using the stile and keep a careful eye to the right where clay pigeons are fired from a shelter. Cross a second gate by a stile then follow the track uphill through pleasantly lonely pasture. The track runs between an avenue of stunted, windblown trees but you may have to skirt round to avoid yet more boggy ground. As you top the skyline, a row of trees leaning precariously east show how exposed this high farming country is.

The track ends at a gap in the fence. Join the metalled road and continue south to the second turning right,

Aerial view of Cathkin Braes with big wood in foreground.

which leads to High Mains Farm. Go past the farm and down a track between an avenue of fir trees that heads towards the houses of East Kilbride. You now pass a mound, the remains of the original Mains Castle, which belonged to the powerful Comyn family. It was lost after John, the Red Comyn, was stabbed to death by Robert the Bruce in 1306. The manner of the killing, before an altar in Dumfries, was shocking even for those harsh times, but it caused a strong national upsurge in support of Bruce which led to his crowning.

A short distance on is the impressive, restored tower of the second Mains Castle. This belonged to the Lindsays of Dunrod in Ayrshire who flourished in great wealth until the last owner's lavish lifestyle forced the sale of the estate to pay off his debts. Mains Castle is the home of Mike Rowan, better known to many people as Big Rory, the

giant bagpipe-playing Highlander on stilts who entertains tourists at festivals around the world. Mr Rowan is also a corporate entertainer, laying on Scottish nights for visiting foreign executives. About 100 m downhill from the castle, work is under way to recreate the old castle loch for windsurfing and dinghy sailing.

Follow the track downhill to the new road that skirts recently built houses at Stewartfield. The track used to continue to the Carmunnock Road but has been obliterated by the new road. Follow this new road, keeping to the top of the embankment until you find a gap in the fence, just before the roundabout beside the Safeway supermarket.

The gap leads back to the Carmunnock Road. Follow this round a left-hand bend then immediately take the road to the right. After about 400 m you reach a crossroads. Cross over and walk about 100 m along a farm track until you come to a gate. Walk across the field until you approach the right-hand corner where the fence meets a line of trees. Cross the fence to get to a track which leads to High Flat Farm. Follow the hedge on the left and head downhill to meet a row of trees at right angles.

You can now reach the more obvious track to High Flat Farm. The farm's speciality is cattle so the going can be rather muddy. Join the tarmac road which passes through the farm and meanders west, passing the dilapidated perimeter fence of a reservoir. The Strathclyde Water sign says 'No trespassing or unauthorised fishing, picnics and bathing strictly prohibited', which presumably means 'Keep Out'.

At about a mile from High Flat Farm you rejoin the B759 less than 400 m from the laybys.

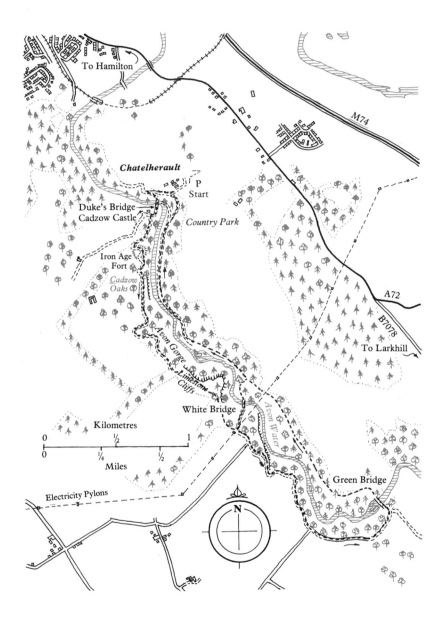

To Hamilton

M74

Chatelherault

P
Start

Duke's Bridge
Cadzow Castle

Country Park

Iron Age
Fort

*Cadzow
Oaks*

A72

B7078

To Larkhill

Avon Gorge

*Limestone
Cliffs*

White Bridge

Avon Water

Kilometres

0   ½   1

0   ¼   ½

Miles

Green Bridge

Electricity Pylons

N

CHATELHERAULT

Like all fairy tale settings, Chatelherault offers a beautiful castle (well, hunting lodge), an enchanted forest, and a morality tale with a happy ending.

Our story begins in 1548 when James Hamilton, 2nd Earl of Arran, received the French Duchy of Chatelherault for arranging the betrothal of the young Mary, Queen of Scots to the Dauphin of France. Almost 200 years later his descendant, the 5th Duke of Hamilton, built a hunting lodge, named after the Duchy, on the outskirts of the town of Hamilton. In the early 1800s the 10th Duke, the enormously proud and wealthy Alexander, 'Il Magnifico', turned the ancestral palace into the most splendid stately home in Scotland, and later built a massive mausoleum (easily seen from the M74 motorway).

Move to the 12th Duke, who lost so much of the family's coal mining fortune at the gambling table that the palace became undermined and had to be demolished. Chatelherault itself was threatened by mining and was a shell when acquired for the nation in 1968. While restoration was going on, national bodies purchased surrounding land, including the beautiful Avon Gorge, and the country park finally opened in 1987. The park is managed by Hamilton District Council.

INFORMATION

Distance: 6 km (3.75 miles).

Start and finish: At car park beside Chatelherault hunting lodge. In Hamilton, follow A72 Lanark road for about 3 km then turn right into the country park.

Terrain: Mainly good paths. Strong footwear advised in wet conditions.

Refreshments: Cafe at Dobbie's Garden Centre nearby.

Public transport: Trains from Glasgow Central to Hamilton Central. From bus station next door, Whitelaws Coaches services to Larkhall and Lanark pass the park entrance.

Opening hours: Chatelherault Visitor Centre: Apr-Sep daily 1030–1730, Oct-Mar 1030–1700. The house is open daily 1030–1615 (closed Christmas and New Year). Ranger service tel: 01698 426213.

Wood sorrel on rotting tree trunk.

Chatelherault, designed by William Adam, has been described as little more than a facade. True, the broad frontage concealed a shallow space occupied by kennels, banqueting hall and Duke's apartment. Nevertheless, there were sumptuous Georgian interiors which were painstakingly restored.

The lodge and grounds were designated a country park in 1987, and about 300,000 people now visit every year. Such a number implies that a quiet walk is out of the question. Nothing could be further from the truth. As the senior ranger, Malcolm Muir, explained, the Avon Gorge must be the only area in this part of Lanarkshire that lies out of sight or sound of industry.

The gorge walk is best done anti-clockwise, beginning by the west wing of Chatelherault.

Chatelherault hunting lodge.

Follow the path that leaves the small car park and heads west for a short distance before swinging downhill to the Duke's Bridge, which towers 80 ft above the heavily wooded Avon Gorge.

Cross the bridge and walk past Cadzow Castle, medieval stronghold of the Hamiltons. A high fence prevents access to the unstable ruins, but in the 16th Century the castle was almost unique in Scotland for its early use of a more ruthless deterrent: wide gunports to allow artillery to sweep vulnerable approaches. Sir

Walter Scott wrote a ballad celebrating Cadzow, but its most famous moment was when Mary, Queen of Scots rested there in 1568 after her escape from Lochleven Castle and before her forces were routed at Langside.

The path soon passes an iron age earthwork, which probably had timber houses within two banks and a ditch.

Next are the celebrated ancient Cadzow oaks, remnants of the last surviving Norman hunting forest in Scotland. Until recently it was thought the oaks were no more than 400 years old, but research work by a Glasgow biology teacher, Martin Dougall, suggests that at least one oak may be 800 years old and others possibly at least 600 years.

Wildflowers

The path continues for some way with fields on the right and forestry plantations on the left. Post-war forestry grants led to a third of the old woodlands being replaced by commercial timber, mainly spruce and larch. According to Malcolm Muir, the move was a mistake. Hamilton District Council wants the emphasis to swing back to traditional, high quality woodland dominated by ash, elm and hazel, with oak on higher, dry ground.

Unfortunately, bad forestry management in the past, the planting of many commercial trees on steep slopes and the selling-off of land to proprietors who would expect compensation for tree-haulage damage means the trees have virtually no economic value.

Nevertheless, small-scale extraction may be carried out, possibly using horses as a visitor attraction. Meanwhile a management plan for the gorge is being prepared and a bird census has been done as part of a full biological survey.

The path on this eastern side of the gorge stays mainly on the level, high above the Avon Water. Glimpses down moss-covered banks to the thickly wooded base of the gorge summon up thoughts of remote

Appalachian valleys where whisky is home-made. Dangerous place for a revenue man! The gorge was in fact a refuge for Covenanters who fled from the battle of Bothwell Brig in 1679. Anne, Duchess of Hamilton, insisted that pursuing troops should not enter her woods.

About halfway along the path, a line of pylons indicates where the White Bridge crosses the Avon. Groups with young children can join the opposite bank at this point and return to Chatelherault, knowing that their shorter circuit still reveals the essence of this beautiful valley.

The path becomes more stoney towards the Green Bridge. A very large beech tree dominates one viewpoint.

The path eventually heads downhill to the Green Bridge, a new wooden structure, suspended in the middle, which was named after an old green metal bridge at the same spot. Cross the bridge and follow the path which enters a plantation and meanders uphill.

Grey squirrels may be seen running across the path. Fifteen years ago only red squirrels were in the gorge but in the last year or so, greys, with their ability to exploit a wider range of food sources, pushed the reds out completely.

On the return, it is worth turning down to the White Bridge, a wooden footbridge on masonry and brick supports. Previous bridges were used to carry coal out from a drift mine. Back on route, the path enters its most beautiful stage, descending to the riverbank. On part of this delightful stretch, with limestone cliffs opposite, steel baskets filled with rock shore up part of the bank.

Severe erosion has occurred farther downriver. The riverside path, which passes under the Duke's Bridge, was closed after heavy rain in early 1994 caused a landslip, bringing down trees. The route continues by the higher path, giving a view to the Duke's Bridge, before returning, via a flight of steps, back to Chatelherault.

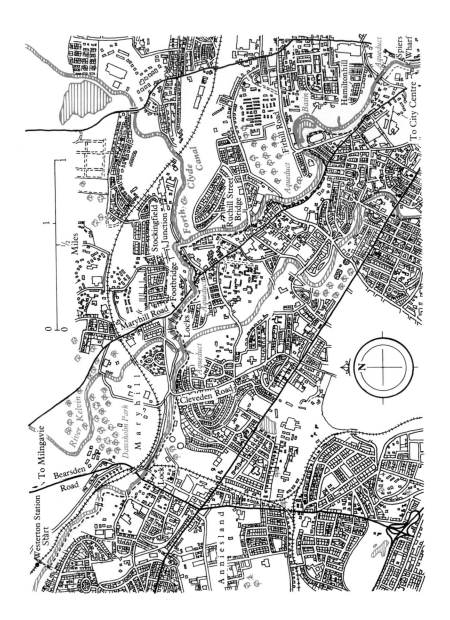

THE FORTH AND CLYDE CANAL

The Forth and Clyde Canal was once the fastest way that Glaswegians could get to Edinburgh – if they so desired. Now, however, the canal is one of the city's best kept secrets. The stretch through Glasgow, where boats passed on their way between the firths of Clyde and Forth, is now the haunt of serene swans, sweaty joggers and the occasional local who uses the towpath as a short-cut between districts such as Maryhill and Anniesland.

Plans for a canal to take small transports and warships across the trim 'waist' of Scotland instead of by the tedious and often dangerous route round the north coast were suggested in the reign of Charles II. But it was not until 1768 that work on cutting a 35-mile channel began at Grangemouth.

INFORMATION

Distance: 6 km (3.75 miles)

Start: Westerton Station.

Finish: Speirs Wharf.

Terrain: Canal towpath. No special footwear needed.

Public transport: Frequent trains from Queen Street to Westerton.

Refreshments: Lock 27 pub.

Lock mechanism at Port Dundas.

By 1775 the canal had reached Stockingfield, where the Glasgow branch was cut south towards the city centre. Two years later funds dried up and construction was halted until 1786 when the Government agreed to grant money from the rents of estates forfeited by Jacobites. This injection of £50,000 allowed the canal to be completed, and it finally reached Bowling on the Firth of Clyde in 1790. The canal became Glasgow's main trading link until the Clyde was dredged. In 1962, falling income forced the canal's closure.

At Westerton Station, which can be reached from Queen Street Station in the city centre, take the footbridges over the railway line and canal. You are now on the south bank and just inside the Glasgow boundary. Join the tarmac path leading up to the towpath and then head east. For the first 500 m or so the towpath may be lonely but the canal itself is busy with waterfowl, particularly mallard ducks. Early in the year, inquisitive ducklings, exploring the narrow bounds of their new world, can be seen getting a scolding peck from imperious swans. Farther on, the chimney of Dawsholm refuse incineration plant can be seen on the horizon.

Just before Bearsden Road, new houses on the north bank are a sign of new life returning to the canal. Bearsden Road, the main route from Glasgow to Milngavie, Drymen and the eastern shore of Loch Lomond, crosses the canal by a large bascule bridge (which splits in half to allow canal traffic through). Cross Bearsden Road and approach another successful act of faith in the canal's future: the Lock 27 pub. This new pub was built on the site of the old lock keeper's cottage; the locks, which are rotten, are due for renewal.

The route continues for half a mile past a gasworks and over a disused railway before reaching Cleveden Road where the canal goes under a low bridge. Cross the road and rejoin the towpath. Continue on, ignoring a lane that leads off to the right, and come to the civil

engineering piece de resistance of the whole canal:
the Kelvin Aqueduct. It is here that the builders ran
short of money, and little wonder. The aqueduct,
when completed in 1790, was the largest structure of
its kind in Britain. About 400 ft long and over 70 ft
high, the aqueduct's four arches span the wooded
valley of the River Kelvin (see Kelvin Walkway).
The scale of the project was so big that the estimated
£6,200 cost escalated to £8,500.

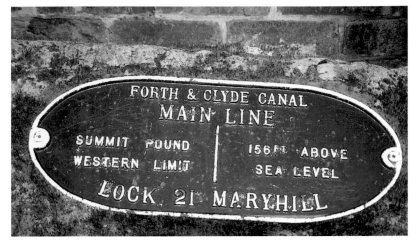

Plaque at Maryhill locks.

Pause on the aqueduct to admire the Kelvin.
Although the track of the disused railway a short
distance downriver is long gone, the uprights of its
bridge still march across the valley and provide
vantage points for a predatory cormorant. Within
200 yards the towpath leads you to another
impressive feat of civil engineering, the Maryhill
locks.

These five locks, which rise like a staircase towards
Maryhill Road, have been scheduled, like the Kelvin
Aqueduct, as ancient monuments. The locks have
been renewed as part of an ongoing programme to
open up the canal again to navigation between
Glasgow and Edinburgh with a footpath and
cycleway also following the route.

This revival has been promoted by groups such as
the Forth & Clyde Canal Society, which organises

cleanups and runs boat trips, and public bodies such as British Waterways and Strathclyde Regional Council who have agreed a development plan for the canal which includes funding and rules which ensure, for instance, that new bridges must allow headroom for boats.

If you want to cut the walk short and continue it another day, you can cross a footbridge at the top of the flight of locks to get to Maryhill Road. Otherwise continue by the canal which crosses Maryhill Road by another aqueduct. To motorists below it must seem inconceivable that waterfowl are paddling about, a few dozen feet above their sunroofs.

About 400 m farther on, you arrive at Stockingfield Junction. Bid farewell to the main canal and turn off down the Glasgow Branch. Pass under Ruchill Street Bridge, a new high-clearance bridge, funded by public bodies including Strathclyde Regional Council and the European Commission. The towpath passes a 19th Century factory building on the opposite bank. Proceed across Bilsland Drive Aqueduct, continue along a stretch with more trees and then walk under another new high-clearance bridge, the 'Nolly Brig', which carries Firhill Road across the canal.

Firhill is home to Partick Thistle, the football team which offers the cuddly alternative to the dour rivalry of Rangers and Celtic. A new wall and land improvements are smartening up what has been a wasteland between Firhill and the canal. As you turn the stadium's last corner, a remarkable view of Glasgow opens up: much of the city's west end, from the elegant sweep of Park Quadrant, above Kelvingrove Park, to the tower of Glasgow University sits in the foreground, and in the distance lie the uplands above Newton Mearns.

Rejoin the towpath as the canal curves south-east past another basin on the opposite bank, and then continue towards Hamiltonhill. Walk by the restored bascule bridge that leads to the Scottish headquarters of British Waterways on the north bank and then continue over the Possil Road Aqueduct.

Soon the towpath becomes cobbled and the dock walls sprout moorings. You have arrived at Speirs Wharf, only about 500 m walk from Sauchiehall Street. On the north bank, opposite, is an imposing terrace of old warehouses, stonecleaned to their original honey colour and converted to flats and business premises. At the far end stands an elegant Georgian building which was once the office of the Forth and Clyde Canal Company.

The actual end of the Glasgow Branch is about 200 m away at North Canalbank Street opposite the Port Dundas Malt Distillery which is easy to find because it has Glasgow's highest chimney. Here, an old, pedestrian bascule bridge and a railway bridge cross the canal. To reach the city centre, return to Speirs Wharf and follow steps down towards the motorway, passing Phoenix Park nursery school on the right. Turn first left and walk under the motorway flyovers towards Cambridge Street where the Hospitality Inn's sign can easily be seen.

Restored warehouses and old Canal Company offices at Speirs Wharf.

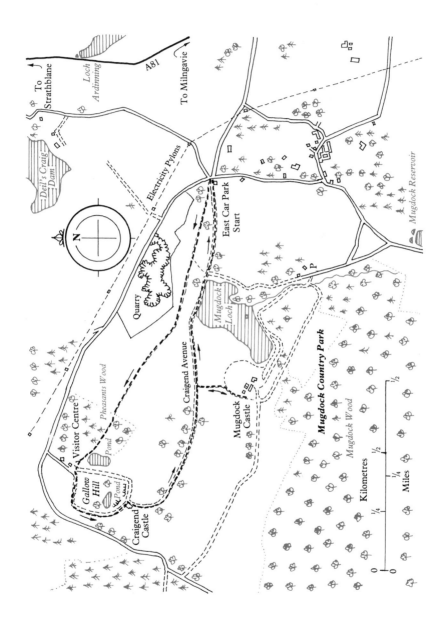

MUGDOCK COUNTRY PARK

Although this walk is short and mainly on the flat, it is packed with interest, particularly for families with young children who will find themselves making repeat visits. Mugdock Country Park lies only two miles north of Milngavie and 10 miles north of Glasgow, making it handy for people who want a short afternoon's jaunt to the countryside. Facilities, include adventure play areas, visitors' centre, and barbecue sites. Paths have been set out for horseriders and cyclists and many paths are surfaced well enough for wheelchairs and prams.

Mugdock, owned by Central Regional Council, was designated a country park in the early 1980s but centuries before it provided macabre entertainment in the form of executions, and there was a zoo in the 1950s. There are two good starting points: The east car park easily reached by turning off the A81 Milngavie to Strathblane road, or the visitor centre about 1 km farther west. The visitor centre is probably best for families with young children as its cafeteria and two craft shops offer rewards for tired, young walkers.

A more scenic start, however, is from the east car park. At the car park, go through a kissing gate and follow the sign which says 'Mugdock Castle and Loch'. On a rough grassy plateau you can see the full sweep of the Campsies to the right, with a particularly good view of the distinctive notch of Dumgoyne.

INFORMATION

Distance: 3 km (1.9 miles).

Start and finish: At east car park of Mugdock Country Park. Take A21 road from centre of Milngavie for 3 km, then turn left and travel 1km to car park.

Terrain: Smooth paths. No special footwear needed.

Public transport: GCT buses service 49 to Mugdockbank then a 1.5 km walk to country park. Or train from Glasgow Queen Street to Milngavie, then Midland Bluebird bus to Balfron/ Strathblane goes within 0.75 km of east car park.

Refreshments: Tearoom, 1100–1730, except winter Wednesdays.

Looking across Mugdock Loch to Mugdock Castle.

Take the most obvious track that swings downhill to the left, following an overhead power line. You now join a straight path that runs alongside, on the right, a low, long, rocky outcrop obscured by rhododendrons and other bushes. This tangle conceals a warren of tracks and hidey holes which children enjoy exploring.

Ignore the path leading left to Mugdock Castle but continue towards the visitor centre. You soon arrive at a small burn, and a tiny waterfall tumbling from a pond. Skirt round the right side of the pond and take the path up to Pheasants Wood, which is a cluster of silver birches whose territory has been invaded by rhododendrons.

The visitor centre, next to Pheasants Wood, is in the 18th century stables of nearby Craigend Castle. Major renovation work, including the rebuilding of the stable block tower and creation of a children's 'discovery' room was expected to end by December 1994. An audio-visual interpretation centre was planned for 1995.

Craigend Castle, an ostentatious mock-baronial house, was built by the Smith family who had acquired the estate, including the Gallowhill, from the Grahams of Mugdock.

Rotting tree on Gallow Hill.

The Smiths had for many generations been tenants and servants of the Grahams. An interesting footnote is that although the family's tie with the estate ended in the 1850s, a business offshoot, the Glasgow bookseller John Smith & Son founded 100 years earlier, is still trading successfully. From the visitor centre take the path past the children's adventure play area to Gallowhill, a wooded knoll. Here, male culprits were 'worreit' or strangled on a gallows and women were 'drounit' in the drowning pond at the foot of the gibbet.

After drownings went out of style, the pool became the water supply for the now ruined Craigend Castle. Craigend was also the site of a zoo which was opened in 1949 and boasted Charlie, said to be the biggest elephant in the world. About 600 m south, but not on the route described here, is the site of a second world war anti-aircraft gun emplacement.

From the roofless and forlorn Craigend Castle, follow the path, Craigend Avenue, that leads east towards the much older Mugdock Castle. At a signposted junction you turn right and follow a causeway of sleepers across boggy ground towards the castle, on a commanding hillside beside Mugdock Loch.

Wildflowers

Mugdock Castle, like Craigend Castle, is a ruin and unsafe to go near, but work has started to stabilise it so that it may be opened as an interpretation centre by 1996. The castle may have been built in the late 13th century, but a deed signed in 1372 is the first written indication of its existence. It is believed the castle was originally protected by a moat drawing water from the loch. The moat no longer exists, but the square south-west tower is the best preserved part of the original stronghold.

The castle was attacked twice in the 1640s. That was when its most famous resident, James Graham, 5th Earl of Montrose, was in prison or leading his army of Irish and Highlanders across mountain passes to achieve stunning victories against his Covenanter enemies. In more sedate times, a walled garden, a Georgian house and then a Victorian mansion (the latter linked to the south-west tower by an aerial walkway) were built in the castle grounds.

South of the castle you can explore Mugdock Wood, where a mixture of old alder, oak, elm and other broadleaved trees grow. This is a Site of Special Scientific Interest (SSSI) because it is regarded as one of the best examples of ancient Scottish woodland.

From Mugdock Castle, go back over the causeway of sleepers to Craigend Avenue and turn right. The route now passes Mugdock Loch, a haunt of herons, coot and tufted duck. Beyond the loch, the route continues for a further, attractive, quarter mile to the east car park.

Tufted Duck

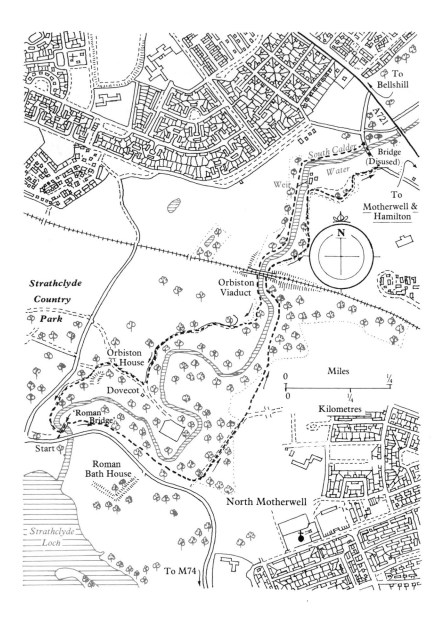

To
Bellshill

A721

South Calder

Water

Bridge
(Disused)

Weir

To
Motherwell &
Hamilton

N

Strathclyde
Country
Park

Orbiston
Viaduct

Orbiston
House

Dovecot

Miles
0   ¼
0   ¼
Kilometres

'Roman
Bridge'

Start

Roman
Bath House

North Motherwell

Strathclyde
Loch

To M74

STRATHCLYDE COUNTRY PARK

Strathclyde Country Park is so well known as an important outdoor sports and leisure centre that it seems hard to believe it could also be a haven for wildlife and a place where people could enjoy a quiet walk in natural surroundings.

In terms of attractions and layout, the park is many-sided. It straddles the M74 Glasgow-Carlisle road with Motherwell to the north and Hamilton to the south. From the motorway the park's most prominent feature, the man-made Strathclyde Loch, can be seen. The loch has an international standard rowing course which was used for the Commonwealth Games in 1986.

Other facilities such as a golf course, sports grounds and a jogging trail help make the park the fourth most visited attraction of its kind in the United Kingdom with a staggering six million-plus visitors recorded annually. Away from the throng, however, there are indeed places where official starters and stopwatches do not hold sway. In the park's 1,650 acres are large areas of wetland, woodland and nature reserves. The park service has two birdwatching hides which can be used, by permit only, by members of the public.

INFORMATION

Distance: 4 km (2.5 miles).

Start and finish: Car park beside site of Roman Fort on Strathclyde Country Park's spinal road. On M74, exit on Junction 5 and drive 1.8 km to car park on south side of spinal road. From car park, walk back north-west along spinal road to Roman Bathhouse.

Terrain: Good paths and tracks. No special footwear needed.

Refreshments: Cafe at the park visitor centre, at the south-east corner of the loch.

Public transport: Train from Glasgow Central to Airbles Station, Motherwell. From station, buses to Hamilton, East Kilbride or Glasgow pass park entrance.

Sandstone cliff.

One walk, the Calder Valley nature trail, begins near the north-eastern end of the loch, within earshot of the cacophonous funfair. Yet this walk can quickly take you deep into a network of footpaths that seem as remote as the legionnaries who used the Roman bathhouse at the start of the trail.

Over 20 years ago the ruined bathhouse was found and fully excavated before the artificial loch was constructed. In the event the water did not flood the bathhouse, as the decision had been taken to move its remains to higher ground in 1980. The bathhouse served the nearby fort guarding the major Roman road through the Clyde valley. Finds from the bathhouse dated it to the Antonine period, after A.D. 140.

Ruins of Roman bathhouse.

From the bathhouse, the trail crosses the park spine road, which carries traffic through the park. Cross to the left bank of the South Calder Water by the so-called 'Roman bridge', actually an old packhorse bridge. A path now winds pleasantly along the riverbank, sheltered by deciduous trees including silver birch and hazel. At this part the South Calder seems more pond than river because it flows lazily by, absolutely flat and quiet compared to the normal run of Scottish burns.

The path soon swings back to the park spine road and runs for about 100 metres along the edge of bushes which follow the line of the road. Turn left up a track, keeping the floodlights of playing fields to your right. You will pass through silver birch trees and hawthorn bushes before coming out beside a housing estate on the right. Follow a gravel track past the houses and return to woodland along a woodland path.

The path descends deeper into the mature woodland. Soon you may detect a looming presence ahead. This is the very high Orbiston Viaduct which crosses the beautiful, wooded valley, carrying the main West Coast rail line down to England. The viaduct is passed under, the track runs high above a gorge and then splits in three. If you take the left track, you will go down to the river where there is a weir. This riverside path goes past a pond on the right and reaches a disused road bridge, which is the furthest limit of the walk.

Weir near end of outward stretch.

An alternative way is to continue straight ahead, following the 'middle' path which soon swings off to the right through rough grassland. At a T-junction, turn left and walk to the bridge which takes you across the river. After crossing the bridge, immediately take a U-turn down to the riverside. The first part of this return leg along the right bank of the South Calder is spoiled slightly by brutal bulldozing of the track. The track soon passes under the massive stone pillars of the Orbiston Viaduct and then goes by a sandstone cliff face rising to the right.

The area around here formed the lands of Orbiston which were gifted in the late 14th Century by Archibald, Earl of Douglas, to the Church. The area became better known in the 1820s when an attempt to establish a co-operative community inspired by Robert Owen's New Lanark failed miserably after about four years. Sarcastic locals christened the community 'Babylon'. Buildings erected for the community ended up being torn down and their stone sold off.

The trail joins a red gravel road which reaches a junction. At this junction is an old dovecot, still with its pigeon holes intact. A left turn leads you down to an old walled garden, now untended, but the trail follows the right turn. The gravel road passes a children's play area and the grounds of the old Orbiston House, base for the community. The grounds are now a neatly trimmed grassy area used for barbecues and games. The track swings round to the left and runs downhill to rejoin the outward route at the Roman bridge.

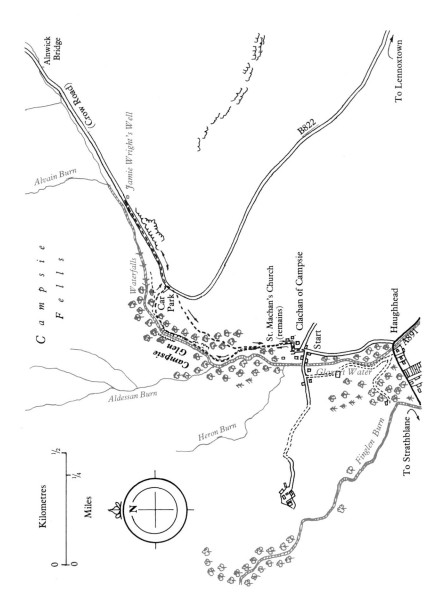

CAMPSIE GLEN

INFORMATION

Distance: 3 km
(1.9 miles).

Start and finish:
Clachan of Campsie
village.

Terrain: Mainly paths,
but small rock
scramble. Strong
footwear with rubber
cleated soles
recommended.

Public transport:
Regular service by
Kelvin Central buses
from Glasgow city
centre.

Refreshments:
Coffee bar at art shop.

For centuries, Campsie Glen has attracted people in search of retreat, rest or recreation. The first famous visitor to what was to become the village of Clachan of Campsie, set beautifully at the foot of the glen, was St Machan, a disciple of Cadoc, the Welsh saint. It is said St Machan brought Christianity to the area and erected a chapel made out of local building materials; turf, wattles, bracken and tree branches.

Another distinguished visitor who arrived from on high, as it were, was the Italian balloonist, Lunardi. After receiving a send-off from a huge crowd in Glasgow, he flew north and landed only a few miles from Clachan of Campsie to a hero's welcome.

Clachan of Campsie really made its name as a place of pilgrimage with the thousands of ordinary working folk from Glasgow who sought a few days of fresh air each year after toiling in the dirty city. The coming of the railway to the area in the 1850s opened up the village to day trippers and large, organised parties.

Looking down on Clachan of Campsie from the Crow Road.

The thing that everyone had come to see was Campsie Glen, a tiny gem of natural beauty hidden away in a fold of the Campsie Fells. The glen is a strikingly attractive gorge formed by the Glazert Water. The glen was originally enjoyed by local people but as word got around, outsiders came flocking. A network of small bridges and ladders, including the famous Jacob's Ladder, allowed even ladies with voluminous dresses to cross the burn and scale rock walls in search of the splendours of the glen.

Campsie Glen.

Even by today's more sophisticated standards, it is still easy to see why people took delight in Campsie Glen. Although the walk through the glen is very short, less than a kilometre, it packs a lot into its distance. There are sheer cliffs covered with vivid-green mosses dripping water droplets on your head. There is a wild tangle of boulders and tree trunks in the river. And there is a succession of waterfalls.

The walk begins in the centre of Clachan of Campsie, near the old graveyard with its ruined parish church said to have been built over St Machan's grave. Turn right past the front of the art gallery and the row of neighbouring crafts shops which decades ago formed the Crown Inn, a noted attraction for trippers.

Go round the end of the row and follow a path to a kissing gate which has ugly sheets of rusting corrugated iron attached to it. This, sadly, is something of an omen. Continue through a beautiful beech wood and enter the glen. Stunningly attractive though the glen is, it is hard to avoid noticing the litter that has been dropped along the banks. Even a litterbin shelter from the car park on the Crow Road high above has been pitched downhill to lodge between tree trunks in the river.

The path is muddy in parts and could do with some duckboards to ensure dry feet. Nevertheless the end is

exhilarating, with a clamber up a steep rocky step (tricky for
the inexperienced) and a dramatic look down to a waterfall.
You can continue uphill to the car park and walk up the
Crow Road for about 100 metres to Jamie Wright's Well,
named after a local angler who felt the need to create the
source because of his thirsty excursions to fishing burns.
Return to the car park, watching out for traffic speeding
along the road, and then head down across grassland above
the glen to the beech wood. A track takes you back to the
kissing gate and the Clachan.

It is worth spending a few moments in
the graveyard. Apart from the ruined
church, the most striking feature is the
mausoleum of one of the oldest local
families, the Lennoxes, after whom
neighbouring Lennoxtown was named.
The mausoleum was first built in 1715
with only one storey but around a
century later, Miss Margaret Lennox had
a second storey built as a waiting room
where she could smarten herself up before church services.

Old graveyard, Clachan
of Campsie.

Sad is the tale of the Rev John Collins of Campsie who was
buried in the graveyard after being murdered in 1648. The
murderer was a local laird whose ambition was to marry a
beautiful local woman until the minister arrived on the
scene. The Rev Collins married the fair lady, but paid for
the honour with his life. The villain then wed the bereaved
Mrs Collins, but it is said the couple separated in horror after
the wife learned of her husband's infamy. Now put that in a
soap opera and see if they'll believe you.

The old Crown Inn buildings and the square in front of
them have undergone extensive renovation. The buildings
retain sash windows and the square has attractive new
flagstones. But shiny black bollards and '1993' litter bins, as
well as uniform olive green signs hanging on the buildings,
appear to be symptoms of a virulent strain of 'heritage
disease' which has swept through the village.

Still, if the bug spreads to the litter louts in the glen, that
will be no bad thing.

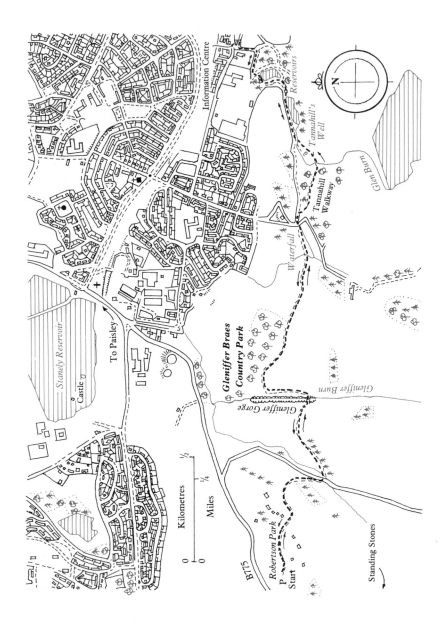

GLENIFFER BRAES

Gleniffer Braes Country Park, a fascinating mix of woodland, scrubland and heathland, is on the southern fringe of Paisley, providing a panoramic view of the town as well as much of the Clyde and beyond.

The park, run by Renfrew District Council, covers about 1,300 acres and has a large network of signed footpaths. This walk begins at the Robertson Park, near the western edge of the country park. The Robertsons in question were the local landowners and famous jam-makers.

On the road up to Robertson Park is the Bonnie Wee Well, immortalised by the 19th century Paisley poet and weaver, Hugh Macdonald: 'The bonnie wee well on the breist o' the brae, That skinkles (sparkles) sae cauld in the sweet smile o' day'. Beside the well is the shell of a hotel. The enterprise failed after its owners assumed wrongly that the council would release land for a car park.

Robertson Park has a car park, viewpoint with picnic and play areas. It is a good access point for the upland Macdonald walks at the park's western edge, standing stones to the south, and a very attractive mix of woodland and water to the east. It is eastward that you are heading. The route leaves the Robertson Park along a tarmac path through high pasture where cows graze.

Beyond the play and picnic areas, a viewfinder points out hills such as Ben Lomond, the Kilpatrick Hills and the western end of the Campsies north of the Clyde. The route soon crosses a minor road and the rest of the Campsies as well as Glasgow can now be seen to the east. On clear days, distant landmarks including the Forth Road Bridge, Tinto in Lanarkshire, Goatfell on Arran and Arthur's Seat in Edinburgh can be seen from the highest points.

The path resumes on the opposite side of the road and continues through a grassy area which has jumping

INFORMATION

Distance: 5 km (3.12 miles).

Start: Robertson Park. Take B775 road from Paisley town centre.

Finish: Countryside rangers' office, Glen Lodge, Glenfield Road, Paisley.

Terrain: Footpaths and tracks. No need for special footwear.

Public transport: Clydeside 2000 bus 24 or 24A from Renfrew Street to Paisley Nethercraigs, which is close to main Glenfield Road entrance to park.

Tannahill's Well.

bars for equestrian events. You next come to Gleniffer Gorge, carved out by the Gleniffer Burn. This is a big attraction, not only for nature lovers but for joyriders who dump stolen cars in the gorge. The problem is being tackled, however, with fencing to prevent more cars going in. In 1993, 15 cars were pulled out of the gorge, and the Army agreed to remove the rest in 1994.

The gorge is so steep and narrow that plant life has been allowed to remain undisturbed. According to the senior ranger, Sarah Bradley, a rare liverwort has been found here. Sarah and her team of two rangers, Dave Powell and Cathy Gillen, have a major and diverse attraction on their hands. The park attracts about 500,000 visitors a year, mostly local people, but also many from farther afield who want to enjoy the outstanding views. Spreading gorse and hawthorn in higher parts of the park attract birds such as the lesser whitethroat, which is on the northern edge of its breeding range. Regeneration of scrubland which is resistant to cows and sheep also attracts large numbers of willow and grasshopper warblers. The high ground is a habitat for curlew and wheater.

Wheatear

The path continues along the 'Tannahill Walkway', named after Robert Tannahill, another celebrated Paisley weaver poet. Tannahill, like Burns, with whom he corresponded, died in his thirties, in 1810. Many of his poems were inspired by walks through the Braes. The wooded Glen Park – which is our destination – features plaques with quotations from his work and a picturesque little stone well (don't drink the water) named after him.

The Braes are not solely associated with romance, however. Ten years after Tannahill's death, the Radical movement was at its height. Provoked by redundancy in skilled trades such as weaving, and Corn Law prices which threatened starvation, Radicals risked death or deportation in forlorn attempts to overthrow the government.

One night in March 1820, a Radical group was arrested in Glasgow. Two hours later, news got through to the

Paisley Radicals' committee who took fright and hid out on the Braes. The Radicals returned home some days later when it was discovered that captured 'incriminating documents' had turned out to be illegible scraps of paper.

Lower Glen Dam.

The walkway gives a clear view of airliners flying in and out of Glasgow Airport, whilst down below the square tower of the probably 15th Century Stanely Castle sits in the reservoir named after it. The site was formerly an island in a marsh before the reservoir was created. The route continues across a second road and into Glen Park woods. Paths through the woods lead down to the picturesque Upper and Lower glen dams which are popular with anglers. The main attraction is the waterfall which tumbles at least 30 ft down a shady, moss-covered cliff. The waterfall can be approached quite safely from below.

Waterfall

The importance of water last century was highlighted by the reluctance of industrial bleachers, brewers and distillers to allow a municipal water supply to be introduced. The industrialists believed the Espadair and Glen burns could meet only their demands but a local doctor, James Kerr, realised there was enough water on the braes for everyone. With the help of the water engineer, Robert Thom, public standpipes giving pure water were turned on in 1838.

Before returning to Robertson Park, a visit to the countryside ranger information centre at the park's Glenfield Road entrance is worthwhile.

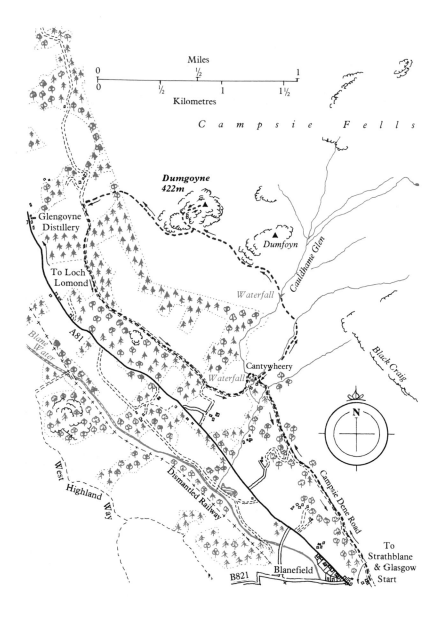

Miles
0   ½   1
0   ½   1   1½
Kilometres

C a m p s i e   F e l l s

Dumgoyne
422m

Glengoyne
Distillery

Dumfoyn

To Loch
Lomond

Waterfall

Cauldhame Glen

Blane Water

A81

Black Craig

Cantywheery

Waterfall

N

West
Highland
Way

Dismantled Railway

Campsie Dene Road

To
Strathblane
& Glasgow
Start

Blanefield

B821

DUMGOYNE

INFORMATION

Distance: 7 km
(4.4 miles).

Start and finish:
Campsie Dene Road,
Blanefield. Parking
prohibited beyond sign
near end of road.

Terrain: Tracks,
becoming steep on
climb to summit.
Strong footwear with
cleated rubber soles
advised.

Refreshments: Cafes
and pubs in
Strathblane area.

Public transport:
Midland Bluebird
service 8 or 10 from
Buchanan Bus Station
to Blanefield.

Opening hours
Glengoyne Distillery:
Conducted tours Mon-
Fri every hour from
1000–1600, Sat
1000–1300. Tutored
'nosing' sessions on
Wednesdays at 1930.

I s it a hill, or is it a mountain? Is it proper to ask such a question about a bit of Scotland that rises only 422 metres above sea level – or 1402 ft in old money? That height does not even qualify for half-Munro status, and there are plenty Munros that do not match the idea that many people have of what a real mountain should be.

What Dumgoyne misses in height, it makes up for in presence. In contrast to the rest of the Campsie Fells which flow smoothly across the rim of the Clyde valley north of Glasgow, this hill rears up like a rhino horn, immediately recognisable from its neighbours. The Campsies in general, along with their neighbours the Kilpatrick and Kilsyth Hills, were formed by lava sheets which were worn down by ice. Dumgoyne, however, was a volcano's vent plug, and its core of hard lava has better resisted weathering.

Dumgoyne, then, is an enigma (maybe a Ben Igma). A hill with attitude, not altitude. It is also a hill to be wary of because the parts that are not covered in potentially slippery grass consist of steep crags or still treacherous little rock outcrops. The fact that a walker died in a fall on Dumgoyne in January 1994 reinforces this point.

Dumgoyne is reached from Glasgow by taking the A81 road to Blanefield, beside Strathblane. In Blanefield, turn right up Campsie Dene Road. This is a private

Looking towards Slackdhu
from lower slopes of
Dumgoyne.

road, and although parking is allowed up to a certain point it should be done carefully, making use of the most obviously parked-on stretches of verge.

As you walk along Campsie Dene Road and pass the last villa on the right, Dumgoyne can be seen ahead, framed by trees. At the end of the road you go through a stiff metal gate and follow an unmetalled road by rough pasture. The route follows this road for about a kilometre, with the cliffs of Black Craig up to the right. A second gate may be locked but a dry stane dyke, beside a Scots Pine, can be climbed. Take care, as there is a wobbly boulder on top.

You go through several more gates, following the road gradually uphill until you come to a house on the left. This pretty, whitewashed cottage with crowstep gables is called Cantywheery. Immediately after the cottage go round a corner and cross a bridge. At a second corner, just up ahead, there is another bridge and a gate with a 'Private Road' sign which also states that dogs should be kept on leads.

Before the second bridge, turn right, go through a gate and follow a track uphill through a field with a conifer plantation on the left and a small rock outcrop looming above. At the top of the conifer plantation, turn left and follow the track towards broadleaved trees. These trees are growing on the steep banks of a picturesque little burn with waterfalls.

Bluebells in Parkhill Wood.

At this point you are heading in the direction of Dumfoyn, Dumgoyne's smaller neighbour. Follow the trees uphill, cross the burn and follow the track to a dyke where stones have been broken down. Cross a fence at this broken section of dyke and continue along the track, past Dumfoyn's lower slopes and on towards Dumgoyne, with Loch Lomond visible in the distance. This stretch of the path gives a good opportunity to consider the best way up Dumgoyne.

You are facing the hill's south flank which has the easiest gradient and simplest routes to the top. Two obvious tracks cross each other on this side of the hill. The easiest track is probably the one that runs from bottom right to top left and then follows the summit ridge to the top. The other leads from bottom left and heads directly to the summit.

The first route is maybe also best because it lets the landscape unfold gradually as you follow the ridge gently to the summit. Initially you will see Conic Hill and Ben Lomond in the distance but at the top much of the Campsies, including Earl's Seat, the highest hill, can be seen spread out to the east.

For descent, it is best to ignore the tracks that lead off the blunt, west side of Dumgoyne. Although they have been used safely on countless occasions, they present a risk because they weave in and out of small rock outcrops. The safest descent is by the easiest way up, but be careful of small pebbles which may act like ballbearings under your feet. Flat-soled trainers are treacherous on grassy or pebbly surfaces such as Dumgoyne's, and lightweight walking shoes or boots should have treads in their soles.

There is a bonus for descending by the easiest way because you can contour round towards the bottom (west end) of the hill and join an obvious track that runs directly underneath the crags. Continue along this track until you are directly above Glengoyne malt distillery on the A81 (visitors welcome).

An obvious track leads downhill to a dyke. Follow the track down to an obvious break in the dyke and cross a fence by a stile. Cross a stream and another fence, again by a stile. Go down an attractive field planted with hawthorn trees to rejoin the unmetalled road back to Cantywheery and then on to Campsie Dene Road. The stretch to Cantywheery passes delightful woodland, crowded with bluebells in spring, and opens out into fields where a view of beautiful, lush Strathblane can be enjoyed.

Following track which skirts below crags at western end of Dumgoyne.

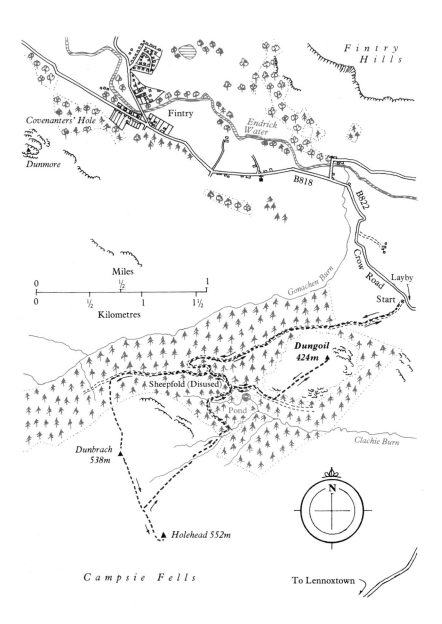

Fintry Hills

Covenanters' Hole

Fintry

Endrick Water

Dunmore

B818

B822

Crow Road

Layby

Start

Gonachen Burn

Dungoil 424m

Sheepfold (Disused)

Pond

Clachie Burn

Dunbrach 538m

Holehead 552m

N

Campsie Fells

To Lennoxtown

Miles

0   ½   1

0   ½   1   1½

Kilometres

DUNGOIL

For such a small hill, Dungoil presents a looming profile above the pretty Stirlingshire village of Fintry. The eastern end of Dungoil is steep and strewn with boulders, presenting real hazards to the walker. Years ago a walk to the top by the gentler westerly slopes would have been easy, but forestry plantations that circle the hill now make the task less straightforward.

This walk includes two very pleasant 'back of beyond' summits, Dunbrach and Holehead. Anyone who wishes to climb only Dungoil can pick it out of the full route. The walk begins at a gate on the Crow Road (B822) from Lennoxtown, less than 3 km from Fintry. The gate is easily found because a sheep shelter stands in the field opposite, on the east side of the road. Cars should be left in a small layby 70 m up the road.

Go through the gate and follow an unsurfaced road uphill to the forest. Go through a second gate, noting Fountain Forestry's fire warning sign. Continue up the road, possibly hearing the screeching cough of pheasants in the trees. After almost 1.5 km the steadily rising road swings round two bends and reaches a junction with forestry post C6 P73. Turn left for Dungoil or right for the full circuit. From this junction look north to the crags below Stronend, the highest of the Fintry Hills.

INFORMATION

Distance: 10.5 km (6.5 miles).

Start and finish: On B822 road 3 km south-east of Fintry (Grid reference NS641849).

Terrain: Considerable amount of climbing on tussocky and occasionally boggy ground. Strong footwear advised.

Refreshments: Pub lunches at Clachan at eastern edge of Fintry.

Public transport: No convenient service.

Top of Dungoil, looking northwest to Fintry.

From the junction, for the full circuit, go right for almost 1 km until a stream crosses the road beside post C4 P73. Follow the stream uphill through a firebreak, which opens up at one point into a pretty but boggy clearing.

On the open hillside, skylarks may be calling. A broad sweep of the Campsies lies open to the west: Earl's Seat and the cliffs of the beautiful Corrie of Balglass on the northern edge of the Fells.

Only 3 km northwest, on the slopes of Dunmore Hill, lies Covenanters' Hole. It was here in 1679 that Covenanters held a conventicle (clandestine religious meeting) only a fortnight after the murder of James Sharp, the minister who had betrayed his fellow Presbyterians by adopting episcopalianism and becoming Archbishop of St Andrews, primate of Scotland.

It is believed that among the worshippers in the hollow was the leader of the group which killed Sharp, John Balfour or Burley, a 'little man, squint-eyed, and of a very fierce aspect'. Soldiers from Stirling surprised the conventicle but no-one was killed in the skirmish. There would be much killing soon after, however, when Burley and the Covenanters defeated John Graham of Claverhouse at Drumclog, and they in turn were beaten with heavy losses at Bothwell Brig.

Further up forestry track.

A short climb, and you are on top of Dunbrach. 'Summit' may be an exaggeration for a swelling on an undulating sea of heathland, but the views now take in Meikle Bin, the Carron Valley reservoir and the Firth of Forth.

The next destination is Holehead. Although this top is less than 1 km to the south, it is out of sight beyond a stone dyke running across the skyline. A map and compass are essential should the weather close in on this featureless terrain. Head for the dyke, and when that drops out of sight, aim to the right of Meikle Bin. The going is very tussocky but you quite soon see where the dyke joins a fence at right angles. Reach the dyke at its western, downhill, end where there is only a fence to cross, therefore no boulders to dislodge.

You can now see the triangulation pillar which is a metre lower than the nearby top. Swing round to the right in your approach to the pillar to avoid the worst of the bogs around the summit pools. From the pillar you can see down to Glasgow and the Clyde Valley.

Retrace your steps, cross the fence again and head towards Dungoil down below. In warm, sunny weather, the walk downhill to the sound of curlews is delightful, but don't let the views draw your attention from drainage ditches underfoot. Aim for where the slopes of Dunbrach and Dungoil seem to converge. The descent becomes steeper between two streams that cut through gullies and join at sheep pens. Join the forestry road at the pens and go downhill, eventually seeing Dungoil through a break in trees ahead.

Wild Primrose

At a junction, another forestry road comes sharply in from the right. Join this second road and go past post C9 P74 and then a pond in a clearing whose water runs into the River Carron near its source. The road now enters a 100 m straight. Halfway along, walk up a narrow firebreak on the left to reach the lower open slopes of Dungoil. After a brief, steep bank, the going is much easier to the top. From Dungoil you can see traffic heading along the Crow Road to and from Fintry. The village was in danger of withering away in the late 18th century until drastic improvements to the old road were made, including reducing gradients.

A suggested descent by the east end should be ignored. Steep grass, particularly in the wet, can be treacherous, and the lower, bouldery ground, is ankle-taxing stuff. The simplest descent is to retrace your steps to the forestry road, turn right and follow the road down through the forest. At both junctions, which you previously encountered, keep straight on, ignoring the roads joining from the left.

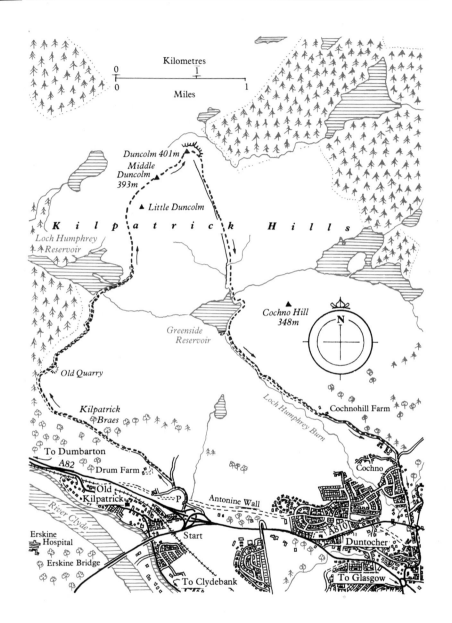

Kilometres

Miles

Duncolm 401m

Middle
Duncolm
393m

▲ Little Duncolm

K i l p a t r i c k   H i l l s

Loch Humphrey
Reservoir

▲ Cochno Hill
348m

N

Greenside
Reservoir

Old Quarry

Kilpatrick
Braes

Loch Humphrey Burn

Cochnohill Farm

To Dumbarton
A82   Drum Farm

Cochno

Old
Kilpatrick

P

Antonine Wall

A810

River Clyde

Erskine
Hospital

Start

Duntocher

Erskine Bridge

To Clydebank

To Glasgow

KILPATRICK HILLS

To hundreds of hillwalkers who head north from the Glasgow area every weekend, the Kilpatrick Hills scarcely rate a second look.

Their neighbours, the Campsie Fells, advertise themselves to motorists with a tusklike Dumgoyne hovering over the highway. The Kilpatricks, however, are more discreet. The Whangie, a magnet for rock climbers, is a hidden cleft in the rolling moorland, and the highest hill, the 401 m Duncolm, presents a benign face to people making their way by the most popular route, from Duntocher beside Clydebank.

Nevertheless, the Kilpatricks are a cherished area. This was shown in 1992 when a plan to develop part of the hillside above Dumbarton collapsed in the face of strong public outcry.

The Kilpatricks are the western end of a chain, also including the Campsies and Fintry Hills, which stretches across central Scotland from Dumbarton to Stirling. Their plateaux were formed from lava. This was mainly basalt in the Kilpatricks, where lava vents created huge stumps of basalt such as Dumbarton Rock and its neighbour, Dumbuck Rock, which (with its quarry) overlooks the A82 road to Loch Lomond and Crianlarich.

INFORMATION

Distance: 11 km (7 miles).

Start: Kilpatrick railway station, Old Kilpatrick.

Finish: Kilbowie Road, Duntocher.

Terrain: Tracks, paths and moorland. Some stretches can be very wet and muddy, so strong footwear is recommended.

Public transport: Frequent trains from Glasgow Queen Street to Kilpatrick. Regular buses from Duntocher back to Glasgow.

Refreshments: Golden Hill pub, Kilbowie Road.

Road following Lord Humphrey Burn down to Duntocher with Glasgow in distance.

The focus of this walk is Duncolm, which is almost exactly at the halfway point of the route. The walk begins at Old Kilpatrick and ends at Duntocher, but it can also be done in two halves, starting and ending at either place with Duncolm as the main objective.

Old Kilpatrick now lies in the shadow of the Erskine Bridge, which was opened in 1971. It replaced the Erskine Ferry, which at one point in the 19th century consisted of a boat which could hold as many as 40 cattle and was pulled across the Clyde on a chain. Now the toll bridge carries tens of thousands of vehicles high over the river each day.

To start the walk, leave Kilpatrick Station in Old Kilpatrick, turn right and walk up the road which passes under the railway line. Follow the road under bridges carrying the A82 road and then take the left fork signposted to Glasgow (the right fork is for Crianlarich).

On Kilpatrick Braes, looking towards Clydebank.

About 400 m from the station, the road enters open country, crossing the line of the Antonine Wall near its western extremity. At this point there is space on both sides of the road for cars to be parked with care. The Antonine Wall, an earth rampart on a stone foundation, was built by the Romans between the firths of Clyde and Forth as a barrier against the tribes in the north. Little of the wall is now visible.

Follow the road as it curves left for a further 300 m and then turn right up a road marked 'Private Road to Houses Only'. Don't be put off by this sign – the road is very popular with walkers, particularly families, who encounter no access problems.

The road climbs steadily up the side of Kilpatrick Braes. The first 400 m, as far as Drums Farm, is on tarmac through deciduous woods. After Drums, the country lane character of the route is left behind and the road becomes a sterner, but still delightful, hill track. As you gradually climb, you will see over your left shoulder the Erskine Bridge vaulting over the

Summit of Duncolm, over-looking reservoirs.

Clyde and the Erskine Hospital for disabled servicemen sitting opposite, on the southern shore.

Avoid a locked gate, with a 'No Dogs' sign, by climbing a stile. As the climb continues, the view becomes even more impressive: Dumbarton Rock rises up to dominate the northern shore while behind, Glasgow sprawls out on both sides of the river. Dumbarton, capital of the old kingdom of Strathclyde, fought Glasgow long and hard over the right to levy customs and dues on ships navigating the Clyde between the mouth of the Kelvin and the head of Loch Long. In 1700, Dumbarton sold the right to Glasgow for the equivalent of £200. At that price, maybe the royal burgh sensed that the future was going to belong to its brash neighbour upriver.

At the top of the Braes, the view opens out further still to encompass Greenock and the hills of Argyll. There's something invigorating about this panorama, which maybe explains why so many of the walkers who make the effort to enjoy it are senior citizens.

The road swings right and continues for 2 km past an old quarry before petering out at the picturesque Loch Humphrey. This is the first of many reservoirs you will see in the Kilpatrick Hills – and no wonder, because the place is one huge sponge.

From the road end, follow a faint track north towards the hummock of Little Duncolm. Stay to the left of this hill and then swing north-east to Middle Duncolm. Ahead lies Duncolm with its triangulation pillar on the summit. Take care while climbing its south-western slope, which is rocky in places.

Duncolm provides the second outstanding view of the walk with Loch Lomond to the west, Ben More to the north, the Campsies to the east and Glasgow and Clydebank to the south. Closer to hand, half a dozen reservoirs ring the hill.

Make your way down the eastern side of Duncolm, and then keep left of a stone dyke that runs south to Greenside Reservoir. A track which runs beside the dyke and then curves round the side of the reservoir is boggy in places and also crosses three small burns. Greenside Reservoir, popular with anglers, is in a pretty setting but a stretch of the track near the dam has been obliterated by heavy clay, pushed down by a bulldozer. This obstacle guarantees muddy, wet footwear so it may be best to climb some distance up the side of Cochno Hill, on the left, to avoid the mess.

Duncolm from the south.

From the reservoir, walk down an unmetalled road towards Cochnohill Farm and eventually Duntocher. This road, by the side of the Loch Humphrey Burn, makes a fitting climax to the walk as its attractive hill farming surroundings contrast sharply with the widening view of the Glasgow conurbation.

The route joins Cochno Road, at the bottom of which is the Golden Hill pub. At the pub turn left and walk a few yards to the roundabout from which Kilbowie Road runs south. On the left (east) side of Kilbowie Road there are bus stops from which frequent Strathclyde buses can be taken to Glasgow.

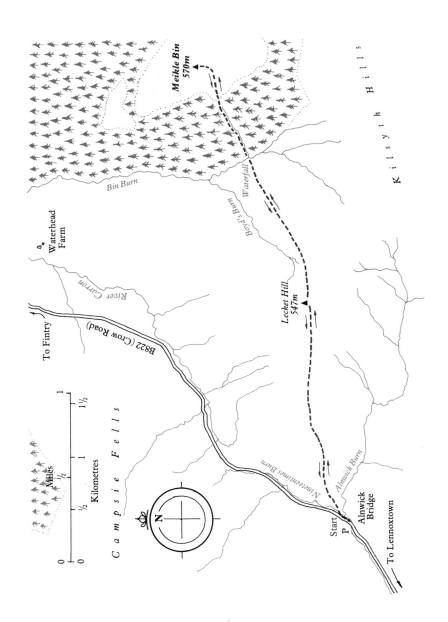

MEIKLE BIN

Overlooking the B822 Crow Road linking Fintry to Glasgow is the 570 m summit of Meikle Bin ('Big Hill'), the highest point of the Campsie Fells east of the Crow Road.

The hill offers the prospect of solitary walking on an attractive, open, undulating landscape and the reward of one of the most fascinating views in Central Scotland.

There are four traditional routes to the top. One starts in the south, relatively low down at Queenzieburn; a second starts north-west of the summit, beside Waterhead Farm, and follows the Bin Burn; and a third comes in from the east, along a road through the Carron Valley Forest.

The route discussed here starts from the Crow Road at the Alnwick Bridge, near the junction of the Alnwick and Nineteentimes burns the map reference is NS 623807 and there are small car parks on either side of the road. This route starts at around 300 m, and is therefore suitable for children embarking on hillwalking careers. The opportunity to 'knock off' Lecket Hill, only 1.7 km from the road, provides a target for youngsters who because of tired legs or bad weather cannot manage the remaining 2.5 km to Meikle Bin.

INFORMATION

Distance: 8.5 km (5.3 miles).

Start and finish: On B822 3.5 km north of Lennoxtown (grid reference NS623807).

Terrain: Tussocky in parts with some small burns to cross. Strong footwear advised. A map (Landranger sheet 64) and compass must be carried.

Refreshments: None en route.

Public transport: Kelvin Central bus from Buchanan Bus Station to Campsie Glen, then walk to start.

At summit triangulation pillar of Meikle Bin, looking towards Carron Valley Reservoir.

This is a hill walk with no signed pathways. The Kilsyth Hills are no strangers to low cloud or mist and the lack of distinct landmarks could cause serious problems in bad visibility. A map and compass are therefore essential, and if there is any suggestion of 'clag' on the tops, then parties with budding junior Munroists would do better to stick to lower walks.

The walk starts by crossing Nineteentimes burn (it apparently needed that number of crossings to follow the burn in a straight line) and taking the obvious track up the steep, broad slope to Lecket Hill. This slope is popular among 'townies' for sledging in winter, as bits of broken plastic in the grass will testify. Height is quickly gained and effort is rewarded (in summer) by skylarks singing only a few feet above your head.

Now on flatter ground, the track, though faint at times, never totally peters out towards Lecket Hill. A view has now opened up: Glasgow to the south and mountains, including Ben Lomond, Ben Ledi and Ben More, to the north. The track leads to two fences which meet at right angles. At each fence there is a stile. Take the right-hand stile and continue to the summit of Lecket Hill, which is marked by a cluster of boulders.

Top of Lecket Hill, looking west in direction of Dungoil.

Meikle Bin can now be seen to the east, its lower slopes almost totally covered by conifer plantations. The best way to the summit is the simplest: trend downhill, aiming for the bottom of the wide firebreak that gives access up through the trees to the summit of

Meikle Bin. By following this route you will descend without having to cross Boyd's Burn to the north or a smaller burn to the south. The smaller burn is best crossed near the bottom of the slope, avoiding its muddy, steep banks higher up.

Climb over a fence and cross Bin Burn just downstream of a picturesque little waterfall. Although care is needed crossing the burn, stepping stones are plentiful. The waterfall flows from a stream that runs down the middle of the firebreak. Clamber up a grassy slope and ascend the firebreak, keeping the stream to your right.

Skull-shaped rock in bed of burn running down firebreak leading to summit of Meikle Bin.

The going now is slightly awkward, with tussocky grass and small drainage ditches running across the firebreak. When you reach another break that runs across the hillside, cross to the right bank of the stream. A short distance up the hill is a piece of wreckage from a Fairey Firefly fighter aircraft which crashed in January 1950, killing two airmen from the Glasgow area.

Quite soon the summit is reached and the view can be enjoyed. And what a view: even in a slight haze, the naked eye can see the Forth Bridge almost 30 miles away; the tall chimneys of the Grangemouth oil refinery are more obvious and the smaller bulk of Stirling University campus can be spotted, glinting white against the dull green of the Ochil Hills.

Below, at the north-east corner of the Carron Valley Reservoir, is the ruin of Sir John de Graham's castle, appearing as a large earthen mound. Farther east, still near the shore of the reservoir, is Kirk o' Muir, early burial ground of the Grahams. Sir John was a friend of William Wallace who died fighting the English at the Battle of Falkirk in 1298. Wallace often sought refuge at the castle.

The return to Lecket Hill and then the Crow Road is done by retracing your steps. Crossing the moor to Lecket Hill, you may be lucky enough to put up a fox sheltering under the bank of a stream.

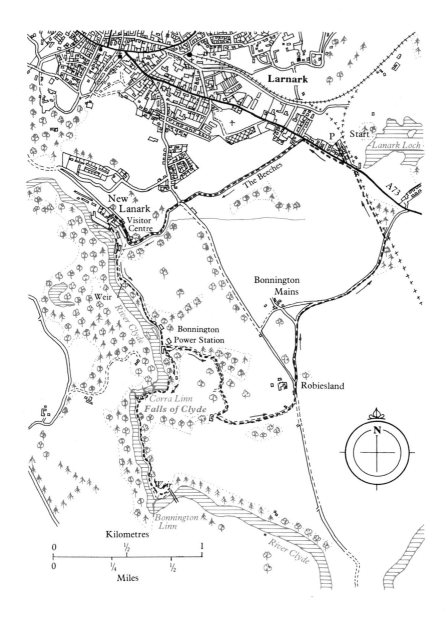

Larnark

Start

Lanark Loch

The Beeches

A73

New Lanark

Visitor Centre

Weir

River Clyde

Bonnington Mains

Bonnington Power Station

Robiesland

Corra Linn
Falls of Clyde

Weir

Bonnington Linn

River Clyde

N

Kilometres

| 0 | ½ | 1 |

| 0 | ¼ | ½ |

Miles

THE FALLS OF CLYDE

This walk is very special because it combines contrasting stretches of outstanding natural beauty with a central feature of industrial history which is still inspiring people from all over the world after more than 200 years.

The walk starts at Lanark Loch, beside the A73 road on the eastern outskirts of Lanark. From the car park go down to the A73, turn right and walk back towards Lanark for about 300 m. Cross the road and turn left down a private unmetalled road aptly called The Beeches. This is a beautiful avenue of large beech trees.

On the skyline to the left is Tinto Hill (see walk 22). After walking downhill for almost a kilometre you come to a crossroads. Go straight over and continue downhill. The track swings left towards a stream before entering a wood. Directly ahead you can see a rooftop.

In a few moments, when you turn right at the bottom of the track, you are standing at the gable end of a long stonebuilt terrace. This terrace was the living quarters for the families who worked at New Lanark, one of the world's largest cotton mills when it was established in 1784 by a Glasgow banker, David Dale, and his partner, Richard Arkwright, the pioneer of mechanical spinning.

INFORMATION

Distance: 6 km (3.75 miles).

Start and finish: Lanark Loch on A73 at eastern edge of Lanark.

Terrain: Paths and tarmac roads. Strong footwear advised in wet conditions.

Public transport: Trains from Glasgow Central to Lanark, then bus to Lanark Loch.

Refreshments: pub lunches at Lanark Loch Hotel. Cafe at New Lanark visitor centre.

Public transport: Train from Glasgow Central to Lanark, then HAD Coaches service 35 to New Lanark.

Opening hours New Lanark Visitor Centre: All year, daily 1100–1700 except Christmas and New Year.

New Lanark: looking towards Dundaff Linn.

The community made its mark on the outside world when Robert Owen was appointed manager in 1798. Owen, who married Dale's daughter, believed that people worked best if they were treated well. His 'social system', which included the chance for children to receive some education, was so ahead of its time that one party of Highlanders, who were set to emigrate to North America, went to New Lanark when they heard about its working conditions.

New Lanark became a showpiece industrial community, with 20,000 visitors turning up between 1815–1825. The mill stopped working, however, in 1968 and the buildings fell into such a state of dilapidation that they were only saved from demolition when a local conservation trust was set up. Major restoration work has included the workers' houses being turned into flats and part of the mills becoming an excellent visitor centre. The large number of foreigners among the tourists who now visit New Lanark testify to the fact that the community is once again a source of interest from abroad.

Much of a day could be spent exploring New Lanark (including the 'Annie McLeod Experience', an audio-visual presentation of what life might have been like in Owen's day) without setting foot near the falls which provided the mills' power. To devote adequate time to this walk, therefore, it is best to enjoy a relatively brief wander past the buildings before setting off upriver, along the Clyde's right bank.

At New Lanark the route starts opposite the centre of the Scottish Wildlife Trust, which runs the Falls of Clyde reserve. Follow 'Falls of Clyde' signs which direct you to the path which firstly runs along duckboards close to the river. Less than 400 m from New Lanark, you find picnic tables placed at an idyllic spot beside a weir.

The path takes you past an attractive old stone cottage and the striking Bonnington power station whose large windows allow you to see some of its internal workings. The hydroelectric scheme here was the first in Scotland to be publicly owned. The path starts to rise above the river and soon the scenic highlight of the walk can be seen: the falls at Corra Linn. The falls tumble down in three main stages, cutting a white, rushing swathe through the surrounding greenery of the woods on either side of the gorge.

Corra Linn.

This prompted Wordsworth to write: 'And yet how fair the rural scene!/ For thou, O Clyde, has ever been/ Beneficent and strong . . .' The falls were painted by Turner and also described by famous writers such as Scott and Dickens. But perhaps the most original perspective was provided by Sir James Carmichael of Bonnington who built a hall of mirrors in a stone pavilion high above Corra Linn. The almost 300-year-old pavilion remains as a ruin, its gaping window staring out at the oak, ash and pine which dominate the woodland, a breeding haunt of a wide variety of birds including chiffchaffs, spotted flycatchers, and great spotted and green woodpeckers.

From Corra Linn there are warnings that much of the path is unprotected, but there are barriers at viewpoints. The upper reaches of the route overlook the deep gorge before descending to the weir at Bonnington Linn. Return to the power station then follow the metalled road that leads up to the right. A short distance uphill, on the left, duckboards have been placed beside a small marsh.

On return leg: beech trees near Bonnington Mains.

The road curves through fields, with impressive Douglas fir growing on the left. Continue past Robiesland and Bonnington Mains farms through another beech avenue parallel to The Beeches. Return to the A73 and turn left to reach the car park at Lanark Loch.

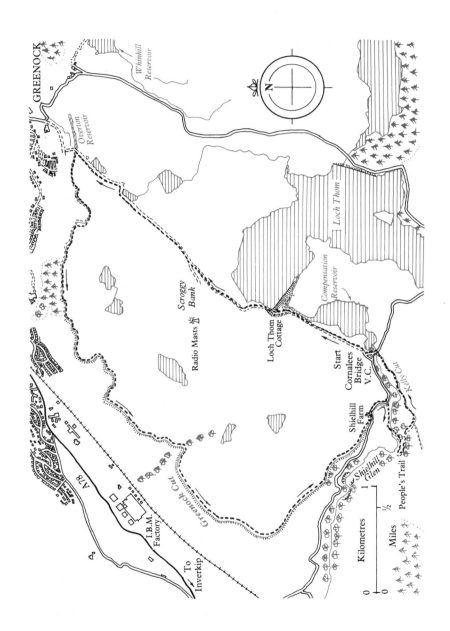

THE GREENOCK CUT

O n this excursion you will start off believing you are an honest-to-goodness walker and end up wondering whether you should claim expenses from whatever is the current equivalent of the KGB. But more of that later.

The walk is essentially about one person, Robert Thom, a brilliant water engineer after whom the starting point, Loch Thom, was named. Greenock, the birthplace of James Watt, was a place of considerable enterprise during the industrial revolution. Shipbuilding, iron production, sugar refining and the making of beer, bottles, soap and even silk hats were among the town's undertakings. As industry spread and the town's population grew, more water was needed to power machinery, and for manufacturing processes and domestic use.

The hills behind Greenock already provided water but Robert Thom believed that the catchment area was large enough to provide much more. An artificial loch (Loch Thom) was created by diverting the course of small streams. An aqueduct (the Greenock Cut), almost 8 km long, was then cut down the side of the hill towards Greenock.

INFORMATION

Distance: 9 km (5.6 miles).

Start and finish: Cornalees Bridge Visitor Centre (signposted from the road between Greenock and Inverkip).

Terrain: Unmetalled road and track. No need for special footwear except in wet conditions.

Public transport: Nearest is bus service from Greenock to IBM or Overton or Inverkip.

Opening hours Cornalees Bridge Visitor Centre: Summer 1230–2130 or dusk, weekends 1000–2130 or dusk. Winter 1230–1630, weekends 1000–1630.

Following road downhill towards Greenock and Firth of Clyde.

Sluice housed at side of Cut.

When the project was completed in 1827 at a cost of £52,000, new undertakings were set up to exploit power from the rushing water. These included a mill for cleaning rice and coffee, a paperworks, factories for spinning wool and making sail cloth, and (the largest) a cotton mill employing 600 people. The Greenock Cut no longer supplies water. Since 1971, a pipe has taken water from Loch Thom. The cut remains, however, and is scheduled as an ancient monument.

The walk begins at Cornalees Bridge, on the moorland road from Greenock to Inverkip. Here, a new visitor centre, replacing one destroyed by fire, has information and a display about Clyde Muirshiel Park, of which this area is part, and its wildlife. Leave the car park, turn left and walk along the tarmac road beside the small compensation reservoir until you reach Loch Thom cottage. On the left side of the road is a well that was made by members of the 5th Battalion Argyll & Sutherland Highlanders. The work, done in August 1915 whilst the soldiers were in training, could hardly have contrasted more extremely with the task they would soon have to face in the Great War.

Go through a kissing gate, and the road becomes rough. On the skyline to the left are radio masts on the summit of Scroggy Bank. The road wends uphill, gradually giving a better view back over Loch Thom to the Renfrewshire hills (including the highest, the 522 m Hill of Stake) to the south.

As the road reaches the summit and Loch Thom falls out of sight, the Firth of Clyde, with Helensburgh on the northern shore, begins to open up. Farther down the road the lie of the land creates a curious optical illusion. Two small reservoirs at the bottom of the slope appear to be separated from the firth by a narrow strip of land. However, the tops of blue cranes at the Lithgow's shipyard betray the fact that Greenock lies about 450 ft below. Over on the north side of the firth, fanning out from east to west, are the town of Helensburgh, the Gare Loch with its Royal Navy submarine base at Faslane, and Loch Long, cutting its way into the Argyll hills.

Well built by Argyll and Sutherland Highlanders.

This part of the walk gives a glimpse of the navy's giant shiplift at the Clyde submarine base at Faslane (make that payment in dollars, tovarish). The shiplift was designed to raise 16,000 tonne Trident submarines for inspection of their 150 m hulls.

At the lowest part of the walk, about 4 km from the start, the walk reaches the whitewashed waterman's cottage where the Greenock Cut joins the Overton reservoir. Cross a bridge with its date plaques marking the cut's centenary. Turn left and start the gentle climb for 9 km, along the path that follows the left bank of the cut back to its source at Cornalees Bridge.

The walk becomes a promenade along a magnificent balcony as the cut curves round the shoulder of the hillside. Views become even more outstanding, with the firth and the mountains beyond opening up more to the west, and Greenock spreading out below.

Much time is spent passing the IBM factory below – symbolic of the big share the plant holds in world personal computer production. The cut itself was something of a technological marvel in its day: dotted along its length are six stone buildings which house ingenious sluices designed by Robert Thom; they open automatically, to stop the cut flooding after heavy rain.

The need for such a safety measure was highlighted one wet winter's night in 1835 when the Whinhill dam (not built by Thom) burst its banks and flooded the east end of Greenock. About 40 people died and much property was destroyed. More primitive than the sluice buildings are the two stone bothies for the men who kept the cut flowing in winter by chopping and digging free any ice and snow. This work was essential because Greenock's industries had been guaranteed a minimum volume of water.

The line of the cut can be seen for some distance as it forms a divide between grass growing on the lower slopes and heather on the upper. Past IBM, the cut swings more to the south, rising into the open moorland with heather now growing on both sides. Now, with most of its tributary streams downhill, the water in the cut becomes slower moving and weed-choked. The view becomes more commanding, with Dunoon and the Cowal Peninsula to the west. As the path heads inland towards Shielhill farm, you enter woodland which thickens up towards Cornalees Bridge.

Instead of returning directly to the starting point, however, it is worth investigating the woodland below in Shielhill Glen. You can leave the Greenock Cut trail near Shielhill farm and descend into the woods, which are a site of special scientific interest, containing mainly broadleaved trees including oak, ash and silver birch. This short route, the People's Trail, takes you down past a disused sandstone quarry which provided material for many of the finer houses of Greenock. The trail leaves the woods by a boardwalk, joins the Kelly Cut, which fed the Greenock Cut, and arrives back at Cornalees Bridge.

Lower stretch of Greenock Cut.

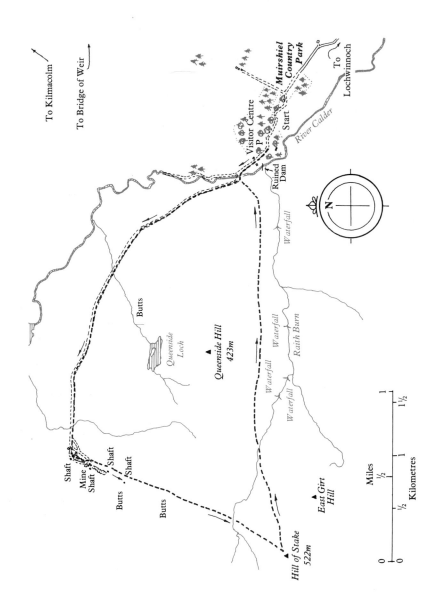

MUIRSHIEL COUNTRY PARK

Muirshiel Country Park is in the heart of the Renfrewshire moorland. In this landscape lurk the ghosts of Covenanters who hid in hollows for their very survival, miners who dug up a mineral used for paper-production and medical diagnosis, and grouse shooters who rode to the butts on their very own train.

The park, which opened in 1970, was the first area to form part of what was to become Clyde Muirshiel Regional Park. The regional park, run by Strathclyde Regional Council in association with Renfrew, Cunninghame and Inverclyde District Councils and local landowners, covers about 30,000 acres and also includes Castle Semple Loch at Lochwinnoch and Cornalees Bridge above Greenock.

This walk takes you out into the moorland from the Muirshiel Visitor Centre, located in attractive woodland in the sheltered valley of the River Calder. The centre, which is about 5 km north of Lochwinnoch, is the base for rangers who provide guided walks for visitors who wish to search out the remains of iron age roundhouses or discover wild flowers, fungi and other hard-to-spot attractions of nature.

The key attraction of this walk, however, is not nature but industry, specifically mining. From the mid-18th Century to 1969 the miners in question dug for a pinkish, red mineral: barytes.

Barytes, which provides the essential pigment in white paint, paper and toothpaste, is obviously much in demand. It also plays an important medical role in barium meals, used to obtain X-ray pictures of the digestive tract.

The 3 km walk to the mines starts at the car park beside the visitor centre. Leave the car park and turn left along the road that runs through the wood. There is a locked gate where the road runs into the open

INFORMATION

Distance: 9 km (5.6 miles).

Start and finish: Muirshiel Country Park, Renfrewshire.

Terrain: Grassy moorland, not too rough but strong footwear recommended.

Note: During the grouse shooting season (12 August to 10 December), the walk to Hill of Stake should not be undertaken without checking with the rangers at the visitor centre that the way is clear. Dogs should not be taken on this walk at any time.

Public transport: None nearer than Lochwinnoch (trains from Glasgow Central).

Opening hours Muirshiel Park Visitor Centre: Summer 1230–2130 or dusk, weekends 1000–2130 or dusk. Winter 1230–1630, weekends 1000–1630.

moorland. Cross over a low fence, taking note of the strict 'No Dogs' sign. The road, which is unmetalled, follows the left bank of the River Calder past a ruined dam and then crosses the river by a bridge, about 150 metres upriver from the dam.

On the right bank, the road continues in a generally north-westerly direction. Along the way you may spot attractive chunks of barytes in the road surface, which is comfortably smooth for most of the way (more than can be said for the potholed tarmac road to Muirshiel Country Park). Little more than 1 km to the north is a spur of an extraordinary miniature railway, built to take shooters onto the grouse moor. About 8 km of track was laid from the 'terminus' near Hardridge Farm.

Derelict mine buildings.

If this walk is done at dusk, the lights of Kilmacolm and Bridge of Weir can be seen from the road as it gains height towards the mines. Evening is a good time to arrive at your destination: the ruined, brick mine building and gaping holes gouged out of the ground create an eerie atmosphere. Metal pipes and bits of old machinery are also strewn on the landscape. Production at the mines reached a peak in the mid-1960s when nearly 17,000 tons of barytes were being excavated annually from deposits as far as 800 ft below ground. Some miners were killed underground, but others died after their lorry left the road in winter.

Walkers are now left with the choice of returning to the car park or taking to the hills – in particular, the 522 metre Hill of Stake, the highest point in Renfrewshire.

The route is on land owned by Strathclyde but let for farming or shooting. Butts between the mines and Hill of Stake reflect the problem presented to walkers during the shooting season. Rangers say that shooting causes no great hindrance in the area though they should be consulted in season.

Even if the way is clear to climb Hill of Stake, you must have a map and compass. Although the distance from the mines to the summit is only about 1.5 km, the moorland is undulating and it is easy to lose the relatively indistinct Hill of Stake among its neighbours unless you are following the map and have a pair of binoculars to spy its triangulation pillar.

From the mines, follow the shooting butts beside a burn, trending uphill and slightly to the left (you are heading south-south-west). The summit should be reached quite quickly as the turf is springy, the heather is mainly short and the sloping ground is generally well drained. On top you are rewarded with a view across the Firth of Clyde to Arran and the Argyll hills.

Track which leads to barytes mine.

Hill of Stake is linked by a fence to East Girt Hill. Head in a south-easterly direction to the lower slopes of East Girt where you may find a small piece of aluminium wreckage from a crashed aeroplane. Continue your descent, keeping to the left of Raith Burn which flows (partly down waterfalls) to Muirshiel Park.

The southern slopes of Queenside Hill, overlooking Raith Burn, provide comfortable going and give the walker the chance to relish the solitude that is now becoming hard to find on well-trodden Munros. Humans can be so scarce that it is possible to startle a solitary deer in the gloaming. Once you have arrived at the River Calder, return to the bridge and cross over to walk back to the visitor centre and car park.

Sunset from Hill of Stake.

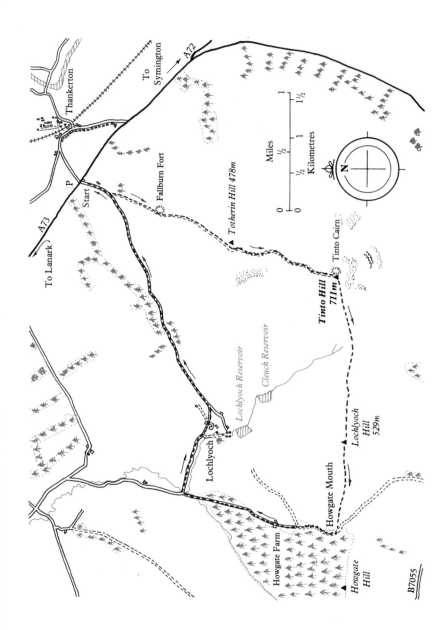

TINTO HILL

There's no escaping Tinto Hill when you visit Lanarkshire's peaceful, rural, upper ward. By Munro standards, the highest point of the Clyde Valley is no giant. When compared to neighbours such as Dungavel Hill or Lamington Hill, however, Tinto is a domineering lump of landscape.

The 711 metre hill rises like a whale above the rich surrounding farmland, and for centuries it seems to have had a magnetic influence. Archeological finds have shown it was a site of ancient worship and burial, and today it still exerts a pull on people who simply wish to get some exercise and enjoy the view from its summit. The walk described here follows the most popular route to the top, but has a different descent.

A car park has been set aside for walkers close to the Thankerton crossroads and a conveniently sited tea room and farm shop on the A73 road between Lanark and Symington. At the car park, go through a kissing gate to reach the moor and follow the obvious track uphill. It would seem that is basically it: keep to the track and follow your nose to the nobbly bit on Tinto's top.

It's not quite as simple as that, however, because the pull up the hill is steeper in some parts than appears from below. Moreover, one moderately steep stretch seems a much harder grind than it actually is because the track has become a wide, gravel thoroughfare disappearing over the horizon.

The lesson with Tinto is to remember that this hill presents about 500 m of climbing in less than 3 km. Done in a rush, that can be heartbreaking stuff, particularly for young parties. But the climb gives constant pleasure if done at a steady pace with pauses to enjoy the unfolding landscape. The lower stages of the track can be boggy where a couple of streams are crossed, but afterwards the going soon becomes dry and firm.

INFORMATION

Distance: 12 km (7.5 miles).

Start and finish: Car park at Fallburn, 5 km east of Lanark on A73.

Terrain: Good tracks on Tinto, followed by tarmac roads on return section. Parts of route up Tinto are steep. Strong footwear recommended.

Refreshments: Tea room and farm shop at Thankerton.

Public transport: Train from Glasgow Central to Lanark. At bus station next door, take Wilson's Coaches service for Biggar and get off at Thankerton.

Following descent down ridge to Lochylock Hill and Howgate Mouth.

An outstanding highlight of the walk, often missed by walkers, can be found less than a kilometre from the car park. Immediately after a fence which is crossed by a high stile, the ground to the left suddenly rises up. It is all too easy to mistake this for an ordinary hummock, and then walk by. Climb this 'hummock', however, and you will find a very unnatural pattern of circular mounds and ditches.

This is the prehistoric Fallburn Fort which, according to the Royal Commission on the Ancient and Historical Monuments of Scotland, measures 64 m across and is in a good state of preservation. A lay person's study of the fort confirms this, as the thick double ramparts still tower as much as 3 m above the ditches from which their earth was excavated. Ironically, at this point (at about 300 metres) you might see a modern expression of military might, a Tornado strike aircraft, flying by on a low-level exercise.

School group on the summit of Tinto.

The track continues to the subsidiary summit cairn of Totherin Hill and then finally up to Tinto Cairn itself. The summit cairn, roughly 45 m wide and 6 m high, is said to be one of the largest bronze age (2,500–600BC) burial cairns in Scotland. That even allows for the stones that have been added to it in subsequent centuries.

Tinto – the hill of fire – is believed to have been the site of fires lit in honour of a sun god. An old record states that at the base of the hill, a tumulus containing the remains of a headless body was found. Compared to such goings-on, a healthy tramp up Tinto can hardly be thought a sacrifice. The reward at the top, in fact, is considerable. The viewfinder reels off a list of hills that might be seen on a clear day: Dun Rig near Peebles, 30 km to the east; Skiddaw, 100 km to the south; Goat Fell on Arran, 95 km west; and Ben Cleuch in the Ochils, 50 km north.

Leave the summit by heading west, down an obvious ridge towards a forestry plantation at Howgate Mouth. Near the summit cairn, cross a fence and keep to the right of the fence and dyke that run along the crest of the ridge. The upper part of the ridge, like other parts of Tinto which are tramped on, has become largely grass-covered. Nevertheless, heather still covers much of the hill and surrounding moorland, and as you walk down the ridge you may startle a grouse which will utter a staccato 'go-back, go-back'.

The path down the ridge provides easy walking, allowing you to admire the scenery. Just out of sight beyond Howgate Hill, however, are the villages of Rigside and Douglas Water which have been trying to fend off an opencast mining development on their doorsteps. At the bottom of the ridge you have to cross a fence to reach the track leading north to Howgate Farm. Take care on the fence as the top wire is barbed. Do not be tempted to head straight across the moor towards Fallburn, as you will encounter Lochlyoch reservoir where access is restricted.

Friendly native.

The final stage of the walk involves 6 km of tarmac road. This is not as unpleasant as it seems because the road is very quiet and mainly used by locals, who often have a smile or a wave for a stranger.

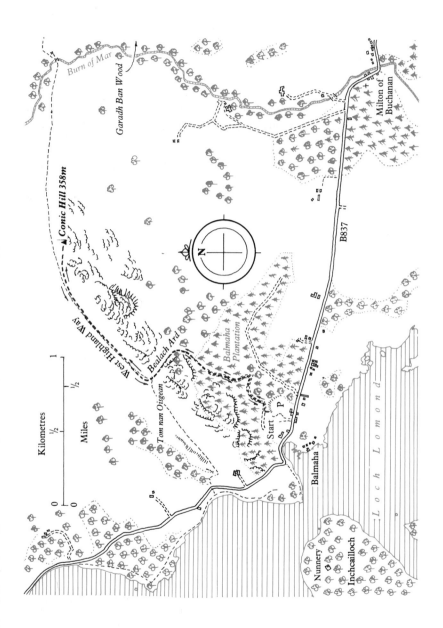

Conic Hill 358m

Burn of Mar

Garadh Ban Wood

Milton of Buchanan

B837

West Highland Way

Bealach Ard

Balmaha Plantation

Tom nan Oisgean

Start P

Balmaha

Loch Lomond

Nunnery

Inchcailloch

Kilometres

Miles

CONIC HILL

For a short day out, there can be few more rewarding places to visit than Conic Hill. The hill is the highest part of the ridge which overlooks the village of Balmaha on the south-eastern shore of Loch Lomond. Though much smaller and less celebrated than big brother Ben Lomond, 11 km farther up the loch, Conic Hill offers its own outstanding views of Loch Lomond and the surrounding countryside.

The 358 m summit of Conic Hill can be reached in less than an hour from Balmaha. This makes the hill an attractive outing for anyone who wants to enjoy a burst of exercise but is pressed for time. Treated with care, the hill should also be within the scope of young children.

Conic Hill is a prominent landmark for walkers following the West Highland Way, which skirts round its northern edge. The hill is near the end of the 1.5 km long ridge which rolls back from Loch Lomond in a series of small humps. Each of these humps provides a good vantage point, but the best of all, obviously, is the highest which gives a commanding view of Balmaha and the inches (islands) of Loch Lomond. The walk begins in the large car park in

INFORMATION

Distance: 5 km (3.125 miles).

Start and finish: Balmaha car park, reached by taking minor road from A81 at Drymen.

Terrain: Forest road then track along part of West Highland Way. Strong footwear advised; care needed on exposed rocks near summit.

Refreshments: Wide choice of cafes and pubs along Loch Lomondside.

West Highland Way, leading up towards Conic Hill.

Balmaha. Join the unmetalled forest road that runs along the back of the car park and turn right. Then follow the West Highland Way yellow indicator arrow through Balmaha Plantation. A short distance on, take a left turn, again following the yellow arrow.

This left turn leads you onto a path which wends its way through the upper section of the wood, which is populated by old Scots pines. Ahead you will see the rounded hump of Tom nan Oisgean, the first prominent top on the ridge. Very soon, the path reaches a boundary fence, with a sign on a kissing gate stating 'No Dogs on Conic Hill'. The reason for the ban is that the path leads out onto hill pasture where sheep are grazing.

Looking down track of West Highland Way towards Inchfad in Loch Lomond.

The instructions continue with a sign from the Loch Lomond Park Countryside Ranger Service which asks you to keep to the marked way, repeats the ban on dogs and adds fires, litter and camping to the list of prohibited activities. On your best behaviour, follow the path round the back of Tom nan Oisgean, through a steep gap called Bealach Ard, then continue on up the path until you are near the back of Conic Hill. A track rises up its flank and leads towards the end of the hill.

The summit is soon gained and you are rewarded with a stunning view of what the Victorians called 'the most beautiful of the Scottish lakes'. Directly below is Balmaha, a small, attractive village with yachts clustered by its shore. Farther out and scattered over the loch are the wooded islands, dominated by the kilometre-long Inchcailloch right under the nose of Conic Hill. This is the 'island of old women', said to be

the site of an ancient nunnery. Too far out for most people to swim ashore is Inchlonaig. This once apparently had a less-salubrious version of the Betty Ford Clinic where people who over-indulged in alcohol were confined and forced to dry out.

Looking northwest towards Inchlonaig in Loch Lomond.

Turning south-east, another sobering thought springs to mind. A few miles away beside the village of Dunblane, John Napier, the person to blame for logarithms, was said to have been born in 1550. For the descent, a variety of tracks lead off Conic Hill. If you are with children, however, it is best to take care as walking down the front can be tricky. Boots have removed surface vegetation, exposing smooth and potentially slippery rock. If you wish to extend the walk rather than retrace your footsteps back down the hill to Balmaha, you can continue east along the West Highland Way. Follow the Way for 2.5 km, crossing the Burn of Mar en route, until you enter the Garadhban Wood and meet the crossroads formed by the road running south from Moorpark.

Turn right and walk a further 1 km down the track to rejoin the B837, which will take you back to Balmaha.

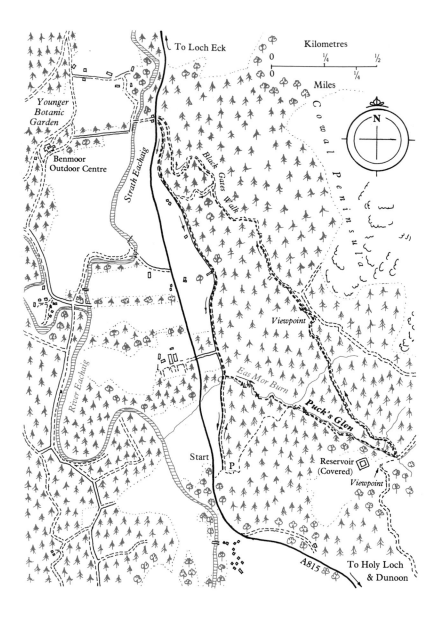

To Loch Eck

Kilometres

Miles

N

Younger
Botanic
Garden

Benmoor
Outdoor Centre

Strath Eachaig

Black Gates Walk

Cowal Peninsula

River Eachaig

Viewpoint

Eas Mor Burn

Puck's Glen

Start

P

Reservoir
(Covered)

Viewpoint

A815

To Holy Loch
& Dunoon

PUCK'S GLEN

This is not cheating! Puck's Glen is indeed about 90 km by road from Glasgow, though about half that distance if you take the ferry to Dunoon. Nevertheless, during the summer months especially, the area which includes Dunoon becomes a sort of Glasgow-sur-Mer.

Cheap package holidays may have killed off mass migrations 'Doon the Watter' to the Clyde resorts, but large numbers of people from the conurbation still need a regular fix of Argyll scenery. Why many do it was summed up hauntingly over 150 years ago by Lord Cockburn, the famous circuit judge. He loved the beauty and serenity of Argyll, with its magical combination of forests, mountains and sea lochs.

He summed up one day thus: 'So we sauntered by the shore – and talked, and gathered shells, and skiffed flat stones on the surface of the sea, and sat on the rocks and lay on the turf, and played with the clear water, and gazed, unceasingly gazed, on the hills, and watched the shadows of the clouds, and observed how the prospects varied with our positions, and with the progress of the sun, and in short had a long luxurious day of repose and enjoyment.' The village of Kilmun on the Holy Loch was described by Cockburn as 'a delightful retreat from the mill, the bank and the bench'.

INFORMATION

Distance: 3 km (1.87 miles).

Start and finish: Forestry Commission car park on east side of A815 Strachur-Dunoon Road, 1.5 km south of Younger Botanic Garden.

Terrain: Good paths and forestry roads. No special footwear needed, but be aware of steep drops beside the route.

Refreshments: Cafe at Younger Botanic Garden. Wide variety of facilities in Dunoon.

Public transport: Train/ferry from Glasgow to Dunoon. Summer bus service from Dunoon to Younger Botanic Garden.

Opening hours Younger Botanic Garden: mid March to end Oct, daily 1000–1800. Other times by arrangement.

Ascending Puck's Glen.

Only 3 km north of Kilmun, lying halfway between the village and Loch Eck, is Puck's Glen. This walk up through the glen – a small, wooded gorge – is one of the best-loved on the Cowal Peninsula. In fact it is one of the most popular walks in the whole of the Argyll Forest Park, established by the Forestry Commission in 1935. The park, the first in Britain, covers 160 sq km and stretches up Loch Goil and Loch Long to include the Cobbler before coming to a halt on the western shore of Loch Lomond just beyond Arrochar. Although Puck's Glen is short, it is packed with delights. The beguiling 'fairy grotto' atmosphere of the gorge through which the path runs should appeal particularly to young children, who should make the ascent easily under their own steam.

The walk begins at the Forestry Commission car park on the east side of the A815, about 1.5 km south of the entrance to the Younger Botanic Garden. From the car park go along the old metalled road that runs parallel to the A815. At the old sign which says 'Dunoon Pier 6 Miles', go through a kissing gate then follow a 'Puck's Glen' sign.

A notice beside the entrance points out that the walk was created in co-operation between the Forestry Commission and the Manpower Services Commission community programme. The walk was originally created in the last century by the landowners, the Youngers brewing family, but had fallen into disrepair. The path was restored in May 1986 with new bridges and other improvements.

The path climbs past a fascinating succession of small cascades and pools, following the route of the Eas Mor (Big Fall) burn. Overhead, water drips and mosses cling to shadowy rocks as the burn rushes by. After less than 500 m the path meets another path which has risen directly from the car park. At this junction, don't lose yourself totally in the scenery; only a few steps away is a steep drop of at least 10 m to the burn.

About 300 m further up, an unmetalled forestry road splits the route. At the forestry road turn right and walk to a viewpoint. Apart from the sight of a concrete-covered reservoir directly below, the viewpoint gives a pleasant panorama over the surrounding woods and hills.

Puck's Glen.

Rather than return down Puck's Glen, you can extend your route to the neighbouring Black Gates walk. This involves continuing north along the forestry road for about 1 km. Along this stretch you come to a better viewpoint which looks across the River Eachaig to the opposite hill, An Creachan. Nestling below An Creachan can be seen the mansion of Ben More, which is now an outdoor centre.

After the 1 km stretch, you will see the sign for the Black Gates walk, leading downhill, back to the old metalled road. On the way down you pass impressive, tall Douglas firs. A short distance downhill you will come to a third viewpoint, and then shortly further on the path splits. The left-hand route descends directly to the road, and the right-hand route veers towards the Younger Botanic Garden on the other side of the river.

The garden, an outstation of the Royal Botanic Garden in Edinburgh, makes a fitting climax to an extended Puck's Glen excursion. The garden has over 200 conifers; some of them belong to rare varieties and are being grown to preserve their genetic strains.

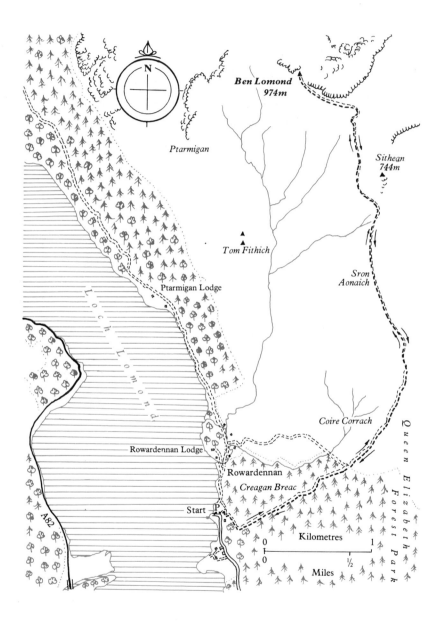

Ben Lomond
974m

Ptarmigan

Sithean
744m

Tom Fithich

Ptarmigan Lodge

Sron
Aonaich

Loch Lomond

Coire Corrach

Rowardennan Lodge

Rowardennan

Creagan Breac

Start

A82

Kilometres

0   1

0

Miles

½

Queen Elizabeth Forest Park

BEN LOMOND

Ben Lomond shares with Ben Nevis and Cairngorm the distinction of being the only big hill that many people will ever want to climb. The other two hills have obvious attractions. Ben Nevis is the highest mountain in Britain, and Cairngorm has a ski lift almost to its summit.

There are more reasons, however, why so many individuals who would never consider themselves hillwalkers make their way up to the 974 m summit of Ben Lomond. The most obvious reason is probably the mountain's beauty: it sweeps up gracefully from the south to its craggy top, then swoops down to Loch Lomond. Ben Lomond's dominating position on the eastern shore of one of Scotland's most beautiful lochs creates a stunning combination.

Another reason is romance. Not only the romance of Rob Roy cultivated by Sir Walter Scott, but also the romance the mountain offered young working-class people during the Depression, many of whom would go on to make a mark in climbing.

A more controversial reason is access. Glaswegians have traditionally looked on Ben Lomond as their hill, and easy access long ago put the mountain on the tourist trail (a guide and pony cost between eight and ten shillings (40–50p) in 1906).

INFORMATION

Distance: 9.5 km (6 miles).

Start and finish: Rowardennan car park, reached by minor road from Balmaha (12 km), on the east shore of Loch Lomond.

Terrain: Forest and mountain path with steep final section. Boots advised. The Landranger map sheet 56 and a compass should be carried. Take good waterproofs and spare food and drink.

Public transport: Shuttle bus, the Loch Lomond Trundler, from Balmaha to Rowardennan in the summer months

Refreshments: Rowardennan Hotel.

Looking south from two-thirds of way up Ben Lomond.

The pressure of pounding feet, increased by Ben Lomond's status as the most southerly Munro (mountain over 3,000 ft/914 m), has brought criticism of the mountain's owner, the National Trust for Scotland. There have been suggestions that NTS should make it more difficult for people to park their cars at the foot of the hill, at Rowardennan. It is hard to see how NTS (who have only owned the mountain since 1983) could ever do this. A century and a half ago, well before the first horseless carriage burst into life, a gazetteer of Scotland said: 'In the summer months, this mountain is visited by strangers from every quarter of the island, as well as foreigners, who come to view the romantic scenery of the highlands'.

Large quartz boulders on skyline near summit.

Virtually anyone who is reasonably fit and allows the time should be able to climb Ben Lomond. Bad weather obviously poses a risk, but although the path is an obvious navigational aid in mist, there seems little point in climbing such a beautiful hill in bad visibility.

From Rowardennan car park, the most popular route of ascent and descent goes past the wooden toilet block shaded by the trees. There is a sign beside the block, indicating Ben Lomond. Follow the path up through the trees. At some steeper sections, care must be taken on rock steps which have been worn smooth by boots. After about 1 km the path reaches the edge of the treeline and leads on to the open hillside where sheep graze. Signs warn that dogs must be kept on leads.

Cross a small bridge and go through a kissing gate. A few yards on there is an NTS plaque on a boulder, marking the start of the Trust's land. At this point you can get a clear view of the task ahead. From here, the path ascends a long grassy ridge for about a further 3.5 km until it reaches the final steep, rocky slope. As you climb, you may notice the temperature getting lower than on the stretch of path through the trees, which can be a suntrap. This change is a reminder of how fickle mountain weather can be, and how advisable it is to carry spare food and clothing.

At a couple of points on the ridge the path zigzags up steeper sections. These offer a good excuse to slow up and enjoy one of the most outstanding views in Scotland. To the south lie the loch's tree-covered inches (islands), Conic Hill above Balmaha on the same shore, and the Firth of Clyde in the far distance. The lobster-claw rock spires of the Cobbler become gradually more obvious to the west.

A lot of work is being done to repair and upgrade the path. Although the clearly defined route may seem an eyesore to some, it does avoid the wide thoroughfare through boggy ground that previously existed. Skill has obviously gone into drainage, paving with small stones (pitching) and following the natural lie of the hill.

Problems in reconciling walkers to the mountain are being echoed on Loch Lomond where attempts are being made to control powerboats and jet skis. There is further controversy about whether the Loch Lomond area, which is a regional park, should become a national park, with funds and legislation to protect the landscape. Critics of national parks say, however, that they have failed adequately to protect areas such as the Lake District.

Back on Ben Lomond, the final steep section presents a steady plod rather than a scramble. Just reward comes at the summit where the view opens to the east and Loch Katrine, which provides Glasgow's water supply, and to the north, other big hills such as Ben Lui and Ben More.

Ben Lomond from west bank.

It will be an unusual day if you enjoy solitude here. In good weather the top will be a honeypot, with walkers seated all around, absorbing the scenery. Don't be surprised to hear foreign voices, particularly German ones. The hill seems to be a perennial attraction to German walkers. Maybe they get EC grants to come here. If that's the case, any chance of one for the Bavarian Alps?

INDEX

Other titles in this series

25 Walks – Deeside
25 Walks – Edinburgh and Lothians
25 Walks – Highland Perthshire
25 Walks – The Trossachs

Other titles in preparation

25 Walks – In and Around Aberdeen
25 Walks – Dumfries and Galloway
25 Walks – Fife
25 Walks – The Scottish Borders

Long distance guides published by HMSO

The West Highland Way – Official Guide
The Southern Upland Way – Official Guide

Printed in Scotland for HMSO by CC. No. 70343 50C 2/95

 **HMSO**

HMSO Bookshops
71 Lothian Road, Edinburgh EH3 9AZ
0131-228 4181 Fax 0131-229 2734
49 High Holborn, London WC1V 6HB
(counter service only)
0171-873 0011 Fax 0171-831 1326
68-69 Bull Street, Birmingham B4 6AD
0121-236 9696 Fax 0121-236 9699
33 Wine Street, Bristol BS1 2BQ
0117 9264306 Fax 0117 9294515
9-21 Princess Street, Manchester M60 8AS
0161-834 7201 Fax 0161-833 0634
16 Arthur Street, Belfast BT1 4GD
01232 238451 Fax 01232 235401

HMSO publications are available from:

HMSO Publications Centre
(Mail, fax and telephone orders only)
PO Box 276, London SW8 5DT
Telephone orders 0171-873 9090
General enquiries 0171-873 0011
(queuing system in operation for both numbers)
Fax orders 0171-873 8200

HMSO's Accredited Agents
(see Yellow Pages)

and through good booksellers